IMAGES
of America

BATON ROUGE CEMETERIES

ON THE COVER: The Baton Rouge National Cemetery was established as a United States National Military Cemetery in 1867. It is adjacent to Magnolia Cemetery. After the 1862 Civil War Battle of Baton Rouge, Union soldiers' bodies were gathered by the troops and buried in the area that would become the National Cemetery. Any Union soldier's body located in Louisiana could be buried in the cemetery, and by 1869, almost 3,000 were interred there. Of those, 494 were unidentified. Baton Rouge photographer Andrew Lytle often captured activities in the National Cemetery, including this worker mowing the grass in the 1890s. (Courtesy of the Andrew D. Lytle Collection, Louisiana and Lower Mississippi Valley Collections [LLMVC], Louisiana State University [LSU] Libraries.)

IMAGES
of America

BATON ROUGE CEMETERIES

Faye Phillips

ARCADIA
PUBLISHING

ISBN 978-0-7385-9184-1

Published by Arcadia Publishing
Charleston, South Carolina

Printed in the United States of America

Library of Congress Control Number: 2012930849

For all general information, please contact Arcadia Publishing:
Telephone 843-853-2070
Fax 843-853-0044
E-mail sales@arcadiapublishing.com
For customer service and orders:
Toll-Free 1-888-313-2665

Visit us on the Internet at www.arcadiapublishing.com

To honor all those who work to preserve the Baton Rouge cemeteries.

Contents

ACKNOWLEDGMENTS

I gratefully acknowledge the assistance provided by Judy Bolton, Jennifer Cargill, Gabe Harold, and Elaine Smyth of the LSU Libraries. I also sincerely thank Kenny Kleinpeter, Chip Landry, Karen Rabenhorst Kerr, Martin Gauthier, Robert Waltman, R.C. and Sissy Albertine, Carolyn Bennett of the Foundation for Historical Louisiana, and the board of the Mid-City Historic Cemeteries Coalition. Thank you for encouragement, technical assistance, editing, and wonderful photographs. Thanks also to the staffs of the Roman Catholic Diocese of Baton Rouge archives department and Roselawn Memorial Park. I wish to thank my editor at Arcadia Publishing, Simone Monet-Williams, for assistance and advice.

INTRODUCTION

Baton Rouge's historic cemeteries exist in a small portion of the city. Originally, Native Americans were buried in mounds on the river bluffs in the area. Of the numerous mounds reported by French and Spanish explorers in the area near the Louisiana State Capitol, only one remains. The first colonial cemetery was established around 1719 on the grounds of the military fort near the Mississippi River. After 1838, the military cemetery was moved to the Native American mound behind the arsenal, and it became known variously as the Military, Protestant, and American Cemetery. In 1931, when the current state capitol building was being constructed, the remains of the cemetery were destroyed. Some graves were reportedly moved to other cemeteries. A sign near the area marks the location of the colonial soldiers' graves, but some believe the men who were buried there actually rest under the green grass of the Capitol Lake banks.

The Catholic Church authorized the first Our Lady of Sorrows Cemetery in 1792. The locations of the first colonial cemetery, Our Lady of Sorrows Cemetery, and the Military Cemetery, are now all part of the grounds of the Louisiana State Capitol. It is here where the journey begins. Approximately five miles south of the capitol is Highland Cemetery, established in 1819 as a Catholic cemetery at the southern edge of what is now the Louisiana State University campus. Lutheran Cemetery's approximate date is 1850, but the date of the first burials is unknown. It is located two and a half miles northwest of Highland Cemetery. Established in 1852, Magnolia is the earliest city cemetery and is adjacent to the Baton Rouge National Cemetery, which officially opened in 1867. They are both approximately two and a half miles from the Lutheran Cemetery. Less than a mile from Magnolia Cemetery are the Sweet Olive Cemetery, established in 1850; the Jewish Cemetery, established in 1858; and St. Joseph's Catholic Cemetery, established in 1826. About two miles east of those is the first perpetual care, park-like cemetery in Baton Rouge, the Roselawn Memorial Park, established in 1926.

Each time development occurred in the areas around the military fort and the capitol, the cemeteries were disturbed, and graves were moved to new cemeteries at the edge of town. Tombstone inscriptions in each existing cemetery indicate the numerous countries of origin of Baton Rouge citizens, such as France, Germany, Italy, and Ireland. St. Joseph's Catholic Cemetery served the Catholics of the city when Our Lady of Sorrows Cemetery closed. St. Joseph's expanded in 1860 and again in 1907, but in 1926, it was closed to burials except for those whose families owned plots with available space. By then, the cemetery was located in the midtown of a growing city. After 1926, parishioners were encouraged to use the newly opened Roselawn Memorial Park Cemetery farther east on North Street. Many families moved loved ones from St. Joseph's and Magnolia to Roselawn at that time. At Roselawn, the grounds were divided into sections for various denominations, including Catholic, Protestant, and Jewish. There are also special sections for Italians and Gypsies, and all religious celebrations are acceptable.

The growing city needed a non-denominational public cemetery. Thus, in 1852, Magnolia Cemetery opened. Leading Protestant citizens were buried there as well as paupers in a section designated for that purpose. When Magnolia Cemetery opened, a number of caretakers of family cemeteries around Baton Rouge brought bodies there for re-interment. Lutheran and Sweet Olive are predominately African American non-denominational cemeteries, and paupers may be buried there as well. The Baton Rouge National Cemetery was created because of the Civil War, and the first burials were for Union soldiers killed in the Battle of Baton Rouge, much of which took place in and around Magnolia Cemetery. Many of Magnolia's grave markers, most notably the one for the Crenshaw children, were damaged. Once the military cemetery was formally recognized, the remaining identifiable graves from the old fort cemetery were moved there. The Jewish Cemetery was established because of yellow fever deaths, and all the cemeteries—except Roselawn Memorial Park—hold victims of the dreaded disease. Not only can names of individuals be found in the cemeteries, but a timeline of events that affected Baton Rouge, such as war, disease, and growth, can also be found within them. The changing city is also reflected in the cemeteries. Family tombs, once well attended, became neglected as the remaining family members died or moved from the city.

Among the more well-known individuals interred at Magnolia are famous Louisiana author Lyle Saxon, Civil War photographer Andrew Lytle, Judge Thomas Gibbs Morgan (father of Civil War diarist Sarah Morgan), and Charles Phelps Manship Sr., publisher of the *State-Times* and *Morning Advocate*. Notable people buried in St. Joseph's are Marie Adrien Persac (1823–1873), important architect, civil engineer, cartographer, and artist; Nathaniel Wells Pope Jr. (1827–1886), West Baton Rouge Parish judge; and the Dudley Turnbull Family, free people of color before the Civil War. Roselawn Memorial Park boasts many notable people including Sen. Russell B. Long, Civil War physician G.H. Tichenor, nightclub pianist Nelrose English Bush, LSU basketball player Albert T. "Apple" Sanders Sr., and historian T. Harry Williams. All the historic cemeteries have lesser known, but well loved, residents.

Downtown—three and a half miles west of Roselawn—on the grounds of the Old State Capitol is the grave and memorial of Gov. Henry Watkins Allen. The journey ends back at the Louisiana State Capitol, where Gov. Huey Long lies under a larger-than-life sculpture. Allen and Long are not buried in actual cemeteries, but their graves are unique to Baton Rouge.

Baton Rouge's early history can be read on the tombstones of its historic cemeteries. Preservation of the cemeteries is the goal of several organizations, including the Foundation for Historical Louisiana, the Mid-City Historic Cemeteries Coalition, the Sweet Olive Cemetery Association, and the Friends of Highland Cemetery. Along with these groups, Rabenhorst Funeral Home and Roselawn Monuments have also restored some grave markers and monuments.

I encourage readers to visit the historic cemeteries. Driving directions to the cemeteries are available on page 127. I hope this book will inspire you to become involved with the preservation efforts of Baton Rouge's historic cemeteries.

One

First Cemeteries

Native Americans built ceremonial and burial mounds near the Mississippi River. In 1542, explorer De Soto and his companions found large villages of hunters and farmers. When the French arrived in 1699, infectious diseases brought by Europeans had decimated the region's once-stable population. Native groups shifted, moved, fought each other, or combined. As pioneers and soldiers arrived in the area that would become Baton Rouge, many of the mounds were destroyed, especially when they were in the path of settlers. French and Spanish Catholics and British Protestants arrived. Catholic church records show that in 1719, clergy from Pointe Coupee came to Baton Rouge to minister to those of the Catholic faith. The British built a small fort in 1763 between the Mississippi River and several nearby Native American mounds that had been constructed around 900 BC.

By 1788, the town had a population of 682. The first cemetery, Our Lady of Sorrows, was established in 1792. Spain supported the rebellious colonies in North America and attacked and captured the British fort. Baton Rouge would remain a Spanish possession until 1810. Early surveys show that the Catholic cemetery on the east side of the fort eventually extended into the garrison grounds. By 1848, the Catholics had stopped burials in the cemetery adjacent to the church, which was rededicated to St. Joseph, and the abutting military and Protestant burial ground was overflowing. Thus, the military established a "new" cemetery, which allowed officers and their families to be buried in a Native American mound overlooking the Mississippi River. Enlisted men and civilians, including slaves, were buried in the lower ground that was prone to flooding from the overflow of Bayou Gracie.

In recounting the history of the military cemeteries, the May 27, 1973, *Baton Rouge Tri-Weekly* laments that a "mass grave of these men, women, and children was never marked," and graves of 300 unknown soldiers and at least two Native Americans were destroyed by construction in 1930–1932. Remains were laid to rest under the foundation and roads of the new state capitol, many of them slaves.

Only one Native American mound still exists on the grounds where the Louisiana State Capitol stands. Because of the overcrowding of the old garrison cemetery, officers were buried in the mound beginning in 1848. Enlisted men were buried on the flood-prone, low-lying ground around the mound. (Courtesy of the LSU Photograph Collection RG A 5000, University Archives, LSU Libraries.)

In 1930, clearing of the old garrison land began prior to the construction of the new state capitol building. Workers found iron coffins marked with English, French, and Spanish coats of arms from as early as 1787. Records indicate that 23 iron caskets were moved to one large grave (pictured) south of the current arsenal museum, but it is unmarked. (Courtesy of the State Library of Louisiana.)

The metal coffins at the old garrison cemetery were similar to this one, which was in a protected area outside the city. In 1991, forensic anthropologists found an unrecorded 19th century burial on the state capitol grounds northeast of the 1838 arsenal, suggesting that not all burials were recovered in earlier excavations. (Courtesy of the Helen Gilkison Papers, LLMVC, LSU Libraries.)

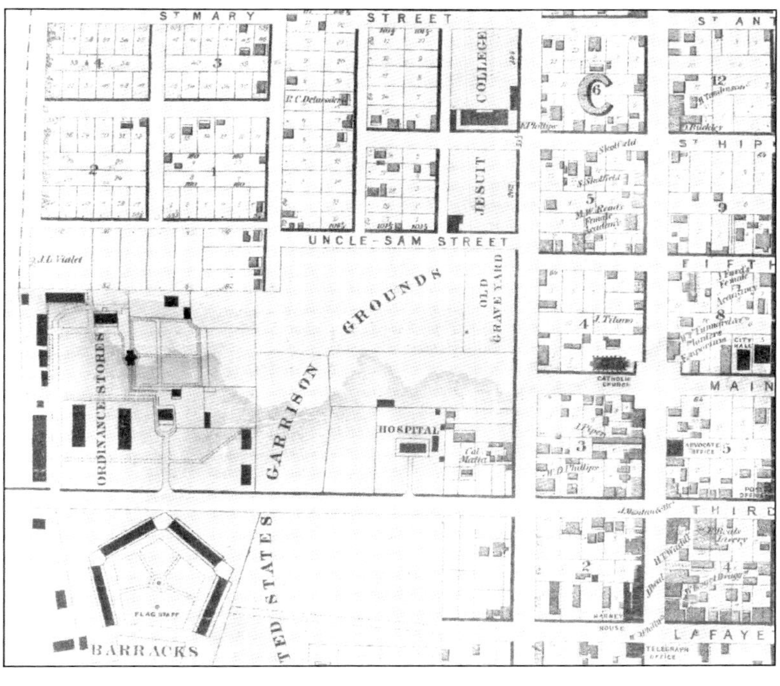

Michael Gill's 1855 map of Baton Rouge shows the United States Garrison Grounds and the location of the "Old Graveyard," which Catholic church and military records indicate was used by both for interments. By 1843, the graveyard shown had fallen into disrepair, and efforts were made to move the graves to the new St. Joseph's Cemetery outside the town limits. (Courtesy of the LLMVC, LSU Libraries.)

Sgt. Edward Hosmer of the 52nd Massachusetts died January 24, 1863, from wounds received at the Battle of Port Hudson north of Baton Rouge. He was buried along with others in the military cemetery on the garrison grounds at Baton Rouge. His brother, Cpl. James K. Hosmer, bought a marble slab for Edward's grave before returning to battle. (Courtesy of the Marshall Dunham Photograph Album, LLMVC, LSU Libraries.)

In 1886, Revolutionary War and War of 1812 patriot Gen. Philemon Thomas was reinterred in the Baton Rouge National Cemetery from the fort cemetery to commemorate the centennial of the American Revolution. The only Revolutionary War battle fought outside the original 13 colonies took place in Baton Rouge. Some of the children and grandchildren of General Thomas are buried in the Highland Cemetery. (Courtesy of the Historic American Landscapes Survey.)

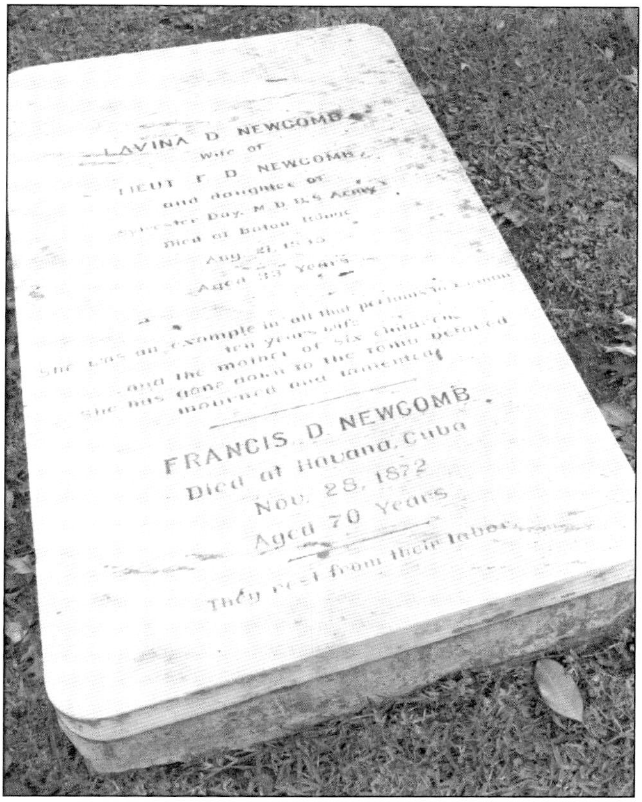

Lavina D. Newcomb died in 1835 while her husband, Francis D. Newcomb, was stationed at the Baton Rouge fort. She was buried in the officers' cemetery near the Catholic Cemetery. Captain Newcomb died in Havana, Cuba, in 1872. His body was returned to lie beside her, and both were moved to the Baton Rouge National Cemetery in 1930. (Courtesy of the Historic American Landscapes Survey.)

Near the entrance to the Baton Rouge National Cemetery are flat markers indicating the 25 graves moved from the garrison cemetery. Some of these men had family members buried at the garrison cemetery. For example, Maj. W.W. Lear had two daughters buried there: Mary Caroline in 1833 and Mary Frances in 1837. (Courtesy of the Historic American Landscapes Survey.)

Confederate veteran Col. David French Boyd served as the first president of Louisiana State University until 1888. Perhaps the last photograph of him was taken in 1898 or 1899 as he and an unidentified cadet planted a tree on the site of the old arsenal cemetery on the far east side of the university campus. (Courtesy of the LSU Photograph Collection RG A5000, University Archives, LSU Libraries.)

A commemorative marker in St. Joseph's Cemetery states: "The first cemetery in Baton Rouge was the cemetery of *La Yglesia de los Dolores de la Virgin*, Our Lady of Sorrows, established in 1792 by order of King Carlos IV of Spain. This monument is erected to their memory by grateful citizens and parishioners in 1991." (Courtesy of the Louisiana Department of Culture, Recreation, and Tourism.)

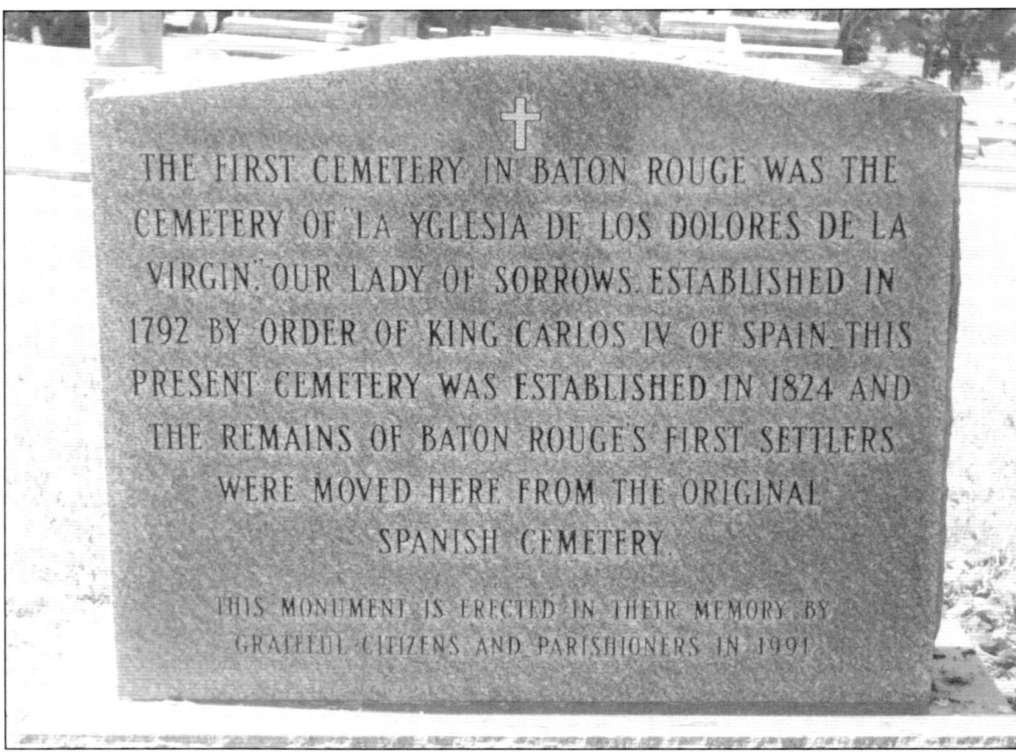

Two

Highland Cemetery

Highland Cemetery is the oldest existing cemetery in Baton Rouge. George Garig, a German settler from Maryland, donated the land for the cemetery to the Catholic Church in 1819. The first burial, however, was that of Capt. John James Neilson in 1813. Since many of the colonists along the bluff around Garig's plantation were German, it became known as the Dutch Highlands and Hill of the Fountains. The Highland Ridge borders Bayou Fountain and extends to Ward's Creek. As early as 1784, Germans and Acadians were settling there. Many of Baton Rouge's first colonists are interred in Highland Cemetery, and two of them arrived in Baton Rouge as a result of the American Revolution. Pierre Joseph de Favrot accompanied Spanish governor Glavez in 1779 when the Spanish captured the British fort at Baton Rouge. He stayed as the commandant of the fort. Gabriel Armand Allard de Duplaniter was an aide-de-camp to French general Lafayette, who aided the Americans. Duplantier remained in the colonies after the war, eventually marrying Constance Rochon Joyce of Baton Rouge and living at Magnolia Mound, her plantation. The priests, unfortunately, kept poor records of the Highland Cemetery, so exact details of many burials do not exist. Some families who are identified include Aubin, Babin, Daigre, Foreman, Kleinpeter, Penny, Randolph, Sharp, and Thomas.

Almost lost to overgrowth and underbrush, the cemetery has been rescued through the efforts of the Historic Highland Cemetery Inc., a group of dedicated volunteers. Led by Evelyn Thom, they began their work as an American Bicentennial project in 1976, and it continues today through the work of Kenny Kleinpeter and the Friends of Highland Cemetery. The Highland Cemetery is located on Oxford Avenue one block east of Highland Road in the first block south of the Louisiana State University campus.

Buried in the Randolph section are Catherine Kleinpeter Randolph (1786–1847), her husband John (1777–1837), and her son John (1818–1856). Also buried there are Ellen M. Smith Randolph (1834–1856), wife of George. They married May 13, 1852. John Randolph (about 1750–1822), father and grandfather of the other Johns, is presumed buried in Highland as well. (Courtesy of Kenny Kleinpeter.)

George Garig, a German settler from Maryland, purchased land on the first natural escarpment above the east side of the Mississippi River from Philip Hicky around 1794. Garig allowed burials on his property as early as 1813, and in 1819, he gave the cemetery to the Catholic Church so that the land could be consecrated. Garig and four of his children are buried in the Highland Cemetery. (Courtesy of Kenny Kleinpeter.)

One of the earliest graves in the Highland Cemetery is that of Elizabeth Sharp Slaughter Davis (1786–1824), wife of William Davis and widow of Ersin Slaughter. Little is known about her. Other Sharp family members may also be in Highland Cemetery, but it is not confirmed. The Sharps are related to the Kleinpeters. (Courtesy of Kenny Kleinpeter.)

Only 12 years old when he died, young Henry Neuville de Favrot's (1835–1847) father, Henri Bouvier de Favrot (1799–1881), was a soldier in the War of 1812 and is also buried in Highland. His family lived in West Baton Rouge Parish, but members of the de Favrot family were traditionally buried in Highland. (Courtesy Kenny Kleinpeter.)

Pierre Joseph de Favrot (1749–1824), a native of France, chose to serve as a captain in the Spanish infantry. He arrived in Baton Rouge in 1779 to participate in the Revolutionary War Battle of Baton Rouge, after which he became commandant of the fort there. He became a US citizen and served in the Louisiana Legislature in 1814. His sons Louis and Philogene served in the War of 1812 for the United States. De Favrot settled his family on a plantation, Monte Vista, in West Baton Rouge Parish, where they became influential citizens. Philogene Joseph was killed in a duel in 1822. De Favrot, his sons, and Louis's unnamed baby—who died in 1824—are also buried in Highland Cemetery. (Courtesy of Kenny Kleinpeter.)

Gabriel Armand Allard Duplantier (1753–1827), a native of France, served as an officer in the French cavalry and came to America as an aide to General Lafayette during the Revolutionary War. Armand served as a commander of US forces in the War of 1812. He and his friend Pierre Joseph de Favrot married sisters Augustine and Francesca (1763–1842) Gerard, respectively. Augustine Eulalie (1788–1876), daughter of Armand and Augustine Duplantier, married Luis Estevan de Favrot (1788–1876), son of Pierre and Francesca. All but Augustine Gerard Duplantier are buried in Highland Cemetery. Joseph Duplantier (died 1864) was the grandson of Armand, and his three young daughters were buried in Highland. Vandals opened their tombs in the late 1930s, after which their remains were moved to St. Joseph's Catholic Cemetery on Main Street. (Courtesy of Kenny Kleinpeter.)

Henri Bouvier Favrot (1799–1881), son of Pierre, served in the War of 1812. He and his wife, Aurore Villars (1809–1877), and their children, Philogene Bernard (1845–1852), Aurore (1832–1911), and Josephine (1840–1913) share the same grave marker. Henri's sister Octavine C. Favrot (1795–1868) is also listed on the marker. Although the inscriptions are in French, the marker was placed sometime after the last death in 1913. (Courtesy of Kenny Kleinpeter.)

Josephine (1785–1826), daughter of Pierre, wrote this poem after her fiancé was killed in the capture of the Baton Rouge fort. Lt. Luis Antonio Boucher De Grand Pre (1787–1810) was the son of the military governor of Spanish West Florida, who was a close friend of Pierre de Favrot. Josephine never married and is buried in Highland Cemetery; Luis De Grand Pre is not. (Courtesy of Kenny Kleinpeter.)

In the 1930s, robbers and vandals destroyed mausoleums and tombs and took burial items. Gravestones were broken and moved, and untended plants grew over tombs, hiding names of the deceased. Descendants of the Favrot family along with the Daughters of the American Revolution, Baton Rouge chapter, attempted to restore order in 1939. (Courtesy of Kenny Kleinpeter.)

"Sacred to the memory of the children of Jefferson P. and Caroline E. Thomas" is inscribed on the tombstone over the graves of Buffington J. Thomas (?), William E. Thomas (?), Antoinette Carolyn Thomas (died 1857), and Florence Thomas (died 1857). They were the grandchildren of Gen. Philemon Thomas. Their parents, Jefferson Plummer and Caroline E. Trager Thomas (c. 1827–c. 1871), are presumed buried in Highland Cemetery as well. (Courtesy of Kenny Kleinpeter.)

Childhood deaths were unfortunately common in 19th century Baton Rouge. Three children born to Therese Addie Rowley (1840–1913) and Oscar Heady Foreman Sr. (1822–1905) died before their parents. Oscar Heady Foreman Jr. (1868–1872) lived the longest. Three-year-old Linda F. Foreman's (1863–1866) grave, along with her brothers, have markers; the graves of their parents, however, do not. Their brother John M. Foreman was born and died in 1862. (Courtesy of Kenny Kleinpeter.)

Joseph Onieda Lopez (1845–1896), a descendant of Alfonso I of Spain, was sent by the king to Louisiana to set up Spanish schools. He became an influential secretary of the Spanish colonial governors. Lopez's descendants lived on a plantation nine miles south of Baton Rouge until a levee break destroyed their home. His children, Henri Lopez (1875–1876) and Anna Euphemie Lopez (1879–1884), were also buried in Highland. (Courtesy of Kenny Kleinpeter.)

Aurelius B. Hodges, son of I.B.A. and Josephine Hodges, died July 17, 1854, at the age of 22. Aurelius is the only member of the Hodges family buried in Highland Cemetery. Nothing is known of his parents, but the lengthy poem on his tombstone, which was expensive to carve, indicates that he was well loved by them. (Courtesy of Kenny Kleinpeter.)

Matilda and Robert H. Penny's names have long been associated with this cemetery as resident owners of a plantation here from 1837 to 1849. They reserved a 30-square-foot family burial plot, where she was buried in 1845 and he in 1849. Also buried here are four children: Lucy Ann and Marian A. in 1846, and Ann W. and James J. in 1850. (Courtesy of Kenny Kleinpeter.)

Rosebuds symbolize the death of a child and are often found on tombstones with the epithet "Budded on Earth to Bloom in Heaven," as seen on this marker for William Ensley Duke (March 26–September 27, 1921). Son of Wiley F. and Mamie H. Duke, his was one of the last interments in Highland Cemetery. No other members of the Duke family are identified in the cemetery. (Courtesy Kenny Kleinpeter.)

Mme. Anne Marie Renee Aime Douezan (1766–1849), widow of Jean Baptiste Riviere and mother-in-law of Francois Gardere, treasurer of the state of Louisiana from 1838 to 1843, owned the Highland Cemetery land in 1826. Madame Riviere was well known in New Orleans society. (Courtesy of Kenny Kleinpeter.)

Charles Daniel Comeaux (1787–1850) is honored for his service in the War of 1812 by a marker from the National Society of the United States Daughters of 1812 over a 20th-century gravestone, which replaced the original that was lost. His son Charles Daniel Comeaux Jr. (1817–1892) is also buried in Highland. (Courtesy of Kenny Kleinpeter.)

Catherine Kleinpeter Randolph (1786–1847), widow of John Randolph (1777–1837), represents both the Kleinpeter and Randolph families whose sections of Highland Cemetery are contiguous. Her husband's grave is nearby, as are those of her brother-in-law Charles Randolph (1828–1856) and other family members. The Kleinpeter plot is enclosed with a wrought-iron fence. The German Kleinpeter family first settled on the highlands in 1784 and became successful sugar farmers at Hard Times Plantation. George was the first to successfully grow sugarcane on the Baton Rouge highlands and was the grandson of Johann George Kleinpeter, the original settler. Many of the other families in Highland Cemetery are related to the Kleinpeters and Randolphs. (Courtesy of Kenny Kleinpeter.)

Many mausoleums have fallen over time, and only bits and pieces remain, such as these blocks that may have been arches. One mausoleum may have contained the graves of Armand Duplantier's wife, Constance Rochon (1766–1841), their son, Didier (1809–1834), their daughter, Euphemie Peniston (1804–1826), and her husband, Anthony (1800–1826), who was murdered a few months after the death of his wife. They left two young children. (Courtesy of Kenny Kleinpeter.)

John Baptist Kleinpeter (1797–1861), captain of the Louisiana Militia during the War of 1812, was the son of George. John Baptiste was the builder of the first steam sugar mill here in 1850, president of the city's bank, and friend of Pres. Zachary Taylor, who once lived in Baton Rouge. His grave is probably in the Kleinpeter section, but the actual gravesite and headstone are lost. (Courtesy of Kenny Kleinpeter.)

The Randolph section is to the left and the Kleinpeter section is to the right, surrounded by the fence. Mary Elvira Kleinpeter Huguet's (1832–1899) funeral ticket states that she was to be buried in the Penny Graveyard, Highland Road, but no marker for her grave has been found. Her husband, John Stephen Huguet (1827–1891), was also buried in Highland, but his gravesite is lost

as well. Huguet was a medical doctor and a veteran of the Confederate military who served in the French Guard. Others in the section without markers could include George Randolph (?), John Randolph (died 1822), Benjamin Franklin Kleinpeter (1845–1858), and Mary Rose Boullion Kleinpeter (1805–1878). (Courtesy of Kenny Kleinpeter.)

The iron fence surrounds at least five graves, and more may be in the plot. Andrew Kleinpeter (1801–1853), son of Joseph, and his wife, Mary Catherine Randolph, had three sons, John Joseph (infant, 1847), Oscar Andrew (1844–1858), and Zachary Pinckney (1849–1857). One obelisk is for Andrew, and the other is for Oscar. (Courtesy of Kenny Kleinpeter.)

The obelisk shown is for Andrew Kleinpeter (1801–1853). He and his two brothers are buried side by side. Sprays of flowers adorn Andrew's obelisk and that of his brother Oscar's, symbolizing rebirth. Infant John's grave is marked by a flat stone. (Courtesy of Kenny Kleinpeter.)

Andrew Kleinpeter's three sons died young, and he is buried with them in Highland Cemetery. This broken footstone may represent the place of rest for his wife and his sons' mother, Mary Catherine Randolph Kleinpeter. The obelisk in the photograph is for Oscar. The inscription states, "To Oscar A. Kleinpeter Died May 28th 1858 aged 11 years and 5 months. He lived as a peaceful dove. He died as blossoms die, and now his spirit floats above, a seraph in our sky." Seraphs are angels that are usually portrayed on tombstones as the winged head of a child. (Courtesy of Kenny Kleinpeter.)

Pierre Joseph de Favrot (1749–1824), Revolutionary War patriot and pioneer settler of West Baton Rouge Parish, is buried in Highland Cemetery. The newly formed Daughters of the American Revolution (DAR) Baton Rouge Chapter placed one of their first markers on Favrot's grave in 1938. H. Mortimer Favrot spoke to the group about his ancestor's life. (Courtesy of the Daughters of the American Revolution Baton Rouge Chapter Records, LLMVC, LSU Libraries.)

The Pierre Joseph de Favrot Chapter of the Children of the American Revolution participated in the 1938 placement of the DAR marker on Favrot's grave. Since then, the chapter periodically has a ceremony to lay a wreath on his grave. The chapter has also replaced the original marker that had been stolen by vandals. (Courtesy of the Daughters of the American Revolution Baton Rouge Chapter Records, LLMVC, LSU Libraries.)

Pierre Joseph de Favrot fought in the 1779 Battle of Baton Rouge against the British, and afterwards, he was appointed commandant of the Baton Rouge fort. His son Philogene served in the War of 1812. Both are buried in Highland Cemetery. In 1938, Favrot descendants and the Daughters of the American Revolution gathered to honor them. (Courtesy of the Daughters of the American Revolution Baton Rouge Chapter Records, LLMVC, LSU Libraries.)

The Baton Rouge Bicentennial Commission and the Foundation for Historical Louisiana placed a plaque in the cemetery listing the names of those believed to be buried in Highland, but whose gravesites were lost. Through the continuing work of the Friends of Highland Cemetery, some of the once lost graves have been found. (Courtesy of Kenny Kleinpeter.)

Three

St. Joseph's Catholic Cemetery

Located on Baton Rouge's Main Street, formerly known as the Comite Road, St. Joseph's Catholic Cemetery opened in 1826. The Corporation of St. Joseph's Church, represented by Armand Duplantier, Philip Hicky, Michael Branagan, and B.T. Beauregard, acting churchwardens, purchased two arpents of land to be used by the corporation as a graveyard. Philip Hicky may be buried in St. Joseph's, but his grave has not been identified. His wife and children are buried there, but none of the other men are buried in St. Joseph's Cemetery.

The cemetery was made available from the beginning to all Catholics—white or black, Union or Confederate, American or non-American. There are 80 Confederate soldiers buried there as well as 21 Union soldiers. Many of the Union soldiers died from disease, not in battle. Since they were Catholic, most of them Irish, their funerals were conducted in St. Joseph's Church. The cemetery was expanded in 1860 and again in 1907, but by 1926, it was closed to burials except for those families who owned plots with available space. Father Glasser encouraged parishioners to use the newly opened Roselawn Memorial Park Cemetery further east on North Street and move their loved ones there. Arrangements were made with Roselawn Memorial Park to allow the same amount of space in the new cemetery as the families had in St. Joseph's. Father Glasser had plans to build a Catholic school on the land where the cemetery sits. A number of families moved graves, and the church moved many priests and nuns to Roselawn into an area established especially for them.

In the 19th century, 600 tombs were erected, and one third of the inscriptions are in French. It was expanded in 1860 and again in 1907, but in 1926, it was closed. By then, the cemetery was located in the midtown of the growing city. (Courtesy of Chip Landry.)

The oldest legible grave marker is that of Lucien Charvet, which reads, "*Neva Grenoble mort le 30 October 1827 age 32 ans bon pere bon ami de lou les gens de bien.*" A broken marker with partial words and church records indicate, however, that Celeste Allain Patin died on October 7, 1827, 23 days before Charvet's death. (Courtesy of Chip Landry.)

Christ looks down on the resting place of Rev. Fr. John Anthony Heil, who died October 19, 1918. Although he worked and died at St. George's Church, he was buried with other priests in St. Joseph's Cemetery. Five of them had died in various yellow fever epidemics in Baton Rouge. Jesuits of the Society of Jesus, they served Baton Rouge from 1849 until 1865. (Courtesy of Chip Landry.)

The crucifix overlooking Father Heil's grave has a plaque that reads, "Katherine Wylie 1914–1935 by her mother Mrs. Jennie Strenzke Wylie." Katherine Helen Wylie is not buried under the crucifix, but rather in the Strenzke family plot. This is a cenotaph, a cemetery monument without a grave beneath. Her mother, Jennie (1887–1974), is not in the Strenzke family plot, but is buried separately. (Courtesy of Chip Landry.)

A gravel path near the front of St. Joseph's Cemetery runs past the Wylie crucifix and shows the variety of the types of graves, monuments, and tombstones used. Repaired tombs can also be seen. In the 1960s, members of the cemetery board moved grave markers while cleaning the grounds and didn't properly replace them, so some markers may be separated from their owners. (Courtesy of Chip Landry.)

A marble headstone for Magloire Bourg (1810–1877) and his wife, Pauline Trahan, was found next to this damaged tomb, but it is not certain if this is where they were buried. During cemetery cleanings, stones were moved and not properly replaced. The tomb has since been restored. (Courtesy of Chip Landry.)

Throughout St. Joseph's Cemetery are tombs of all sizes, shapes, and conditions. Some have received no repair, and others, like the large white mausoleum in the background of this photograph, seem out of place because of their refurbishments. Cypress trees, which are native to the area, have grown up among the graves. This tree was uprooted during a storm and removed from the cemetery. (Courtesy of Chip Landry.)

Shown is an enlargement of the iron cross pictured in the bottom corner of the previous photograph. Iron crosses made by local blacksmiths were common in graveyards throughout southern Louisiana in the 19th century. This one and a smaller one next to it are the only iron crosses still standing in St. Joseph's Cemetery, although many were probably present before the mid-20th century. There are no legible words remaining on the cross to identify whose grave it belongs to, although the cross may have originally been over Farlow family graves. Fifty forms of the cross are utilized in Christian symbolism. The terms "Latin cross" and "Greek cross" refer to the overall proportions of the vertical and horizontal members. A cross with equal bar proportions is considered a Greek cross, and those with unequal bar proportions are called Latin crosses. This one resembles iron crosses made in Germany and Bavaria. (Courtesy of Chip Landry.)

The Verbois family tomb dates from around 1910 and has been repaired and given a white exterior. The brick tomb of Francoise Marie Mela Mernard (1831–1832) and her father, Francois Menard (1783–1838), has not been repaired. The obelisk was erected by the Woodmen of the World in memory of E.D. Verbois (1848–1902). (Courtesy of Chip Landry.)

"Father & Mother" is carved in a unique soaring arch over the other tombs. "Mother" was Eliza LaNoue Larguier (1823–1882). "Father" was Joseph Larguier (1819–1883). The tomb and plot include grandparents, children, and grandchildren. Interred here also is Rosa Larguier (1847–1873), the first wife of Leon Jastremski, mayor of Baton Rouge from 1876 to 1881, and their daughter Estelle Marie Jastremski (1871–1881). Jastremski is buried in a separate plot. (Courtesy of Chip Landry.)

In 1926, the year that three-year-old Mary Louise Barcelona died, she had asked for a dollhouse for Christmas, so the family built her tomb to resemble a dollhouse. Originally, it was painted with a red roof. In the 1990s, Mary Louise was moved to the Barcelona family plot in Roselawn Memorial Park. (Courtesy of Chip Landry.)

Ellen Jane Cothell died on October 9, 1915, at the age of one year and four months. Her mother, Georgia Langhart Cothell (1886–1919), and father, Joseph Sidney Cothell (1876–1933), chose the statue of a little girl reading a book for her tombstone, because she loved books. There are no graves marked with the names of her parents, but the Langhart plot is near her grave. (Courtesy of Chip Landry.)

At right is an example of the extensive deterioration that has occurred to many tombs in St. Joseph's. Below is the tomb after restoration by cemetery sexton Chip Landry. Many families have moved away and can no longer care for their family plots, and the church does not provide care. The grave marker is inscribed, "Melanie Mears, daughter of W.H. Mears and Augustine Verrett, born June 28, 1821, and died June 22, 1839." No one is sure the marker goes with the tomb, but it was stuck in the open end for many years. (Courtesy of Chip Landry.)

A human-sized angel keeps watch over the Strenzke family plot while sprinkling flowers and looks ready to guide them toward heaven. Funerary urns, such as the four in the Strenzke enclosure, are traditional symbols of grief. Rough, unfinished stone, as used on the angel's cross, appears in Baton Rouge cemeteries in the early 20th century. The Strenzke family migrated from Germany to Baton Rouge around 1860. Eight members of their family including parents, children, and grandchildren rest in the plot. The first interred was August Strenzke (1834–1916), "a devoted husband and father," and then his wife, Anna Hein Strenzke (1844–1921), "a devoted wife and mother." Tombstones exist for family members August N. (1868–1950), Edward G. (1881–1944), Mirt D. (1881–1949), and Sam S. (1882–1955). Other children of August and Anna Strenzke were King (born 1885) and Jennie (born 1887). (Courtesy of Chip Landry.)

A roughhewn cross marks the back of the Strenzke family plot's angel. To her right, the back of the tablet with the details of August and Anna Strenzke's deaths is in the same stonecutting style. Crosses and angels in the cemetery represent salvation, mourning, and commemoration. (Courtesy of Chip Landry.)

Joseph De Biendello's (1866–1944) grave is marked with a soldier of God statue carrying a cross that over time has lost its head. The name on the headstone is Joseph D. Biendello, because the English stonemason misunderstood the Italian name. (Courtesy of Chip Landry.)

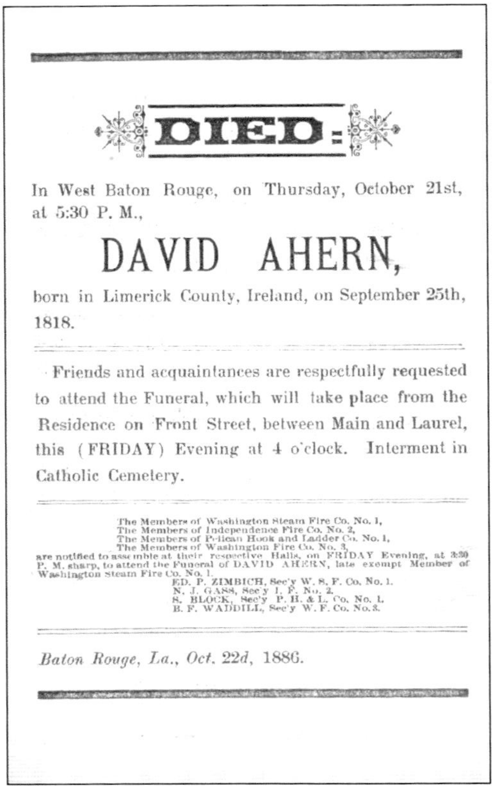

DIED:

In West Baton Rouge, on Thursday, October 21st, at 5:30 P. M.,

DAVID AHERN,

born in Limerick County, Ireland, on September 25th, 1818.

Friends and acquaintances are respectfully requested to attend the Funeral, which will take place from the Residence on Front Street, between Main and Laurel, this (FRIDAY) Evening at 4 o'clock. Interment in Catholic Cemetery.

The Members of Washington Steam Fire Co. No. 1,
The Members of Independence Fire Co. No. 2,
The Members of Pelican Hook and Ladder Co. No. 1,
The Members of Washington Fire Co. No. 3,
are notified to assemble at their respective Halls, on FRIDAY Evening, at 3:30 P. M. sharp, to attend the Funeral of DAVID AHERN, late exempt Member of Washington Steam Fire Co. No. 1.

ED. P. ZIMBICH, Sec'y W. S. F. Co. No. 1.
N. J. GASS, Sec'y I. F. No. 2.
S. BLOCK, Sec'y P. H. & L. Co. No. 1.
B. F. WADDILL, Sec'y W. F. Co. No. 3.

Baton Rouge, La., Oct. 22d, 1886.

From the death notice for David Ahern, it is known that he was a fireman, where and when he was born, when and where he died, where he was living at the time, and that he was to be interred in the Catholic Cemetery. However, it is not known where his grave is located in St. Joseph's. (Courtesy of Baton Rouge Funeral Notices, LLMVC, LSU Libraries.)

Mary and Jesus were late 20th century additions to the Austin family plot. The style of the statues does not match the earlier gravestones and statues. Many of the 19th century markers were carved by local Baton Rouge stonecutter Robert Wiseman, who is also buried in St. Joseph's Cemetery. (Courtesy of *The Catholic Commentator.*)

By 1926, the cemetery was in very poor condition and almost full. Father Gassler encouraged families to move their loved ones to the new Roselawn Park Cemetery on North Street east of St. Joseph's. In 1925, he received a letter from the operators of Roselawn offering local Catholics a designated part of Roselawn for their burials. Father Gassler promised parishioners that they could receive the same amount of land in Roselawn as they had had at St. Joseph's. This cinder block double tomb is that of Stanley Dennis Valdry and his wife, Ophelia. (Courtesy of Chip Landry.)

Beyond the tree, four oven vaults are enclosed in a family pyramidal tomb. In front of the tree are several headstones that appear to be unrelated. To the left is a cross for Elmira Huchenson. On the middle headstone, only the name Rodneys is legible. The headstone on the right is for M. Acosta, wife of A. Barron (1860–1905). (Courtesy of Chip Landry.)

St. Joseph's Cemetery was restricted to burials of Catholics and their spouses, Catholic or not. It was open, however, to all races of Catholics and their families, a rarity in 19th century Baton Rouge. The Dudley Turnbull Family, a free family of color in the 1850s, has a family plot very near those of the white Kleinpeter and Strenzke families. (Courtesy of Chip Landry.)

The Brooks family plot contains the graves of Joseph Brooks (1836–1889) and his daughter Bertha Brooks Addison. Joseph's tombstone states, "In Memory of a Devoted Husband and Father." Bertha (1878–1905) was the wife of Dr. W.P. Addison. She died in Sabine Parish from blood poisoning contracted during childbirth. (Courtesy of Chip Landry.)

Caroline Focken married Charles F. Rabenhorst in 1858. He was a first-generation immigrant from Prussia. According to family legend, he met Caroline either on board the ship from Europe or in New Orleans after he arrived. A rather folksy portrait of Charles depicting him around 40 years old still hangs in the Government Street funeral home. Pictured here is Caroline Rabenhorst wearing a mourning brooch with Rabenhorst's portrait. (Courtesy Karen Rabenhorst Kerr.)

When the Civil War began, Charles F. Rabenhorst, a cabinetmaker, formed his own military company, which became attached to the 21st Louisiana Regiment. In 1864, he moved with his young family to Baton Rouge. In 1866, Charles was building more coffins than cabinets, so he formed the Rabenhorst Funeral Home, which celebrated its 145th year in 2011 as a family owned and operated business. (Courtesy of Karen Rabenhorst Kerr.)

Alvin E. and Oscar F. Rabenhorst, sons of Charles and Caroline, were the second generation to operate the funeral home. Allie Rabenhorst also owned a wood and coal company. Oscar created the first horseless hearse in Baton Rouge for the Rabenhorst Funeral Home on the chassis of a Ford truck, like these, and built the body of the hearse out of wood. (Courtesy of Karen Rabenhorst Kerr.)

Catherine Deremeaux (1827–1900) lived a long life surviving yellow fever epidemics, the Civil War, the aftermath of war, and the loss of her husband. In the 1870 census, her birthplace is listed as Deu, Reine, Germany. Her children were Barbet, John, Mary, Frank, Louis, and Rosa. Her children showed their love through the epitaph "In Loving Memory of Our Darling Mother, May She Rest in Peace." (Courtesy of Martin Gautier.)

In the foreground is the grave of Lawrence Mulvihill (1834–1866), who was born in Ireland, and the family plot of David Pearly Parker, who is buried here with his wife, Delores. Other Mulvihill family members buried in St. Joseph's are his two young daughters, Bridget (1857–1862) and Mary (1864–1866). (Courtesy of Chip Landry.)

Margaret Eberhard of California placed this tombstone for her sister Susanna Baum, "A native of Bavaria, Germany, Born Dec. 24 1824 Died Feb. 1 1903 Ever Remembered Erected by her Loving Sister." In the 1850 census, her husband, Jacob, a baker, and a son, Francis Louis, age 10, are listed as living with her. In 1880, Susanna is listed as divorced and employed as a grocer. (Courtesy of Martin Gauthier.)

Four

Sweet Olive Cemetery

Sweet Olive Cemetery is recognized as the oldest black cemetery in Baton Rouge and is located in the 2200 block of America Street bounded by South 22nd Street, Louisiana Avenue, and Delphine Street. Although some graves in the Lutheran Cemetery may be older, that has not been documented. Few records of the burials were kept in the decades before 1890, and the earliest unmarked burials were probably covered by later burials. In 1898, Sweet Olive was owned and maintained by benevolent societies at two area churches, Mount Pleasant Baptist Church and First African Baptist Church, until 1912. From 1912 to 1975, the property was divided and separately owned by the two societies.

Visitors are greeted at the main entrance on South 22nd Street with an elegant marble sign inscribed with the words, "Sweet Olive Cemetery, circa 1850." Slaves from plantations in the area may have been Sweet Olive's first occupants, as 20th century families have identified graves of ancestors who were slaves. Documented burials of free people of color are in St. Joseph's Cemetery, but undocumented ones may be in Sweet Olive. Many of the city's civil rights leaders and black business pioneers are buried in Sweet Olive as well as veterans of World Wars I and II and the Korean War. Vivian and Fred C. Matthews Jr. formed the Sweet Olive Cemetery Association in 1975 to bring the community together for the preservation of the cemetery and to take over its management. Matthews served as president of the Sweet Olive Cemetery Association until his death at age 95 in 2001. Funds were received from the US Department of Housing and Urban Development to build a brick and iron fence and concrete steps.

In November 2001, the cemetery greeted visitors with signs on either side of the main entrance. On the right was the marble sign inscribed, "Sweet Olive Cemetery, circa 1850," and on the left stood a short wooden post with a typewritten note that stated, "we need money for improvements." In 1998, Roselawn Monument Company donated this marble entrance wall marker. (Courtesy of Kenny Kleinpeter.)

Baton Rouge photographer Rick Albertine named this photograph "Broken Dreams." Albertine captures Sweet Olive Cemetery's beauty and sadness in its disrepair. The mosaic flowerpot on top of the back tomb represents the beauty, and the open and broken tomb in front represents the sadness. (Courtesy of R.C. Albertine.)

Although broken open and scattered with debris, the Dilworth, Davis, and Green family graves are marked with an improvised tombstone. The names are written in a clear and obviously caring hand. Sweet Olive was the city's first incorporated cemetery for black residents and was managed by two local churches, Mount Pleasant Baptist Church and First African Baptist Church. (Courtesy of R.C. Albertine.)

Mr. Elliot's tombstone states, "In memory off [sic] our dear brother Gilbert Martin Elliott who departed this life Nov. 11 1931. We loved you dearly. Sure you know. Jesus called. You had to go." The other standing stone is for James Jackson, "Died Oct 24 [year unreadable] Age 62." (Courtesy R.C. Albertine.)

To the left of the leaning tree is the double tomb of Mother Evella L. Roussel (1861–1917), and Daughter Adell Roussel (1902–1959). The tomb behind them is also for Roussel family members. A variety of metal crosses are placed on graves throughout the cemetery. Most of them appear to have been made in the 20th century. (Courtesy of R.C. Albertine.)

Sweet Olive has always made room for the poor. Parts of it still serve as a potter's field, or a place for unknown or indigent persons buried at public expense. In the Bible, they are referred to as the "friendless poor." Many of the areas for them are unmarked. (Courtesy of R.C. Albertine.)

Many of the graves in Sweet Olive Cemetery are crowded together, cracked, decayed, badly sunken, and unmarked. Others have stones with hand-carved letters. More elaborate markers and urns with mosaic tiles are also prevalent in Sweet Olive. The mosaics are artistic and appear in multiple colors or simply in white. (Courtesy of R.C. Albertine.)

Occasionally, graves are topped with fresh flowers. Fresh paint in traditional white or island colors is often applied. Expensive stone markers are seen next to handmade ones. As of 1991, the five-acre cemetery still accepted burials for people who already had relatives there. Sweet Olive has always been non-denominational. (Courtesy of R.C. Albertine.)

Single and double tombs, some brick, some whitewashed, and others painted with color, seem even more sad with the roots of a withered tree in front of them. Sweet Olive Cemetery is the resting place of many of those who formed the roots of the Baton Rouge African American community in the 19th century. (Courtesy of R.C. Albertine.)

Family members regularly visit graves, especially on religious holidays and Veterans' Day. John Brooks comes yearly to repaint the tomb of his niece's mother and grandmother in preparation for All Saints Day, November 1. Friend Sam Banks sometimes helps him. (Courtesy of R.C. Albertine.)

The tiny cross in the center of the photograph may rest over the grave of a child, although no name appears to identify the deceased. Tombstones for individual children were often made in a smaller size, especially if they were to be placed in cemeteries with limited space. (Courtesy of R.C. Albertine.)

On the wings of an angel, a child is depicted as being borne away to heaven. Though unidentified, the grave is probably that of a child. The motif of an angel carrying a child and dropping flowers is common to Louisiana cemeteries, but the dentil edging is unusual. (Courtesy of Kenny Kleinpeter.)

Many of the city's African American leaders are buried in Sweet Olive, including Rev. Washington Monroe Taylor, a former pastor of Mount Zion Baptist Church; Wesley Ringgold, a prominent businessman; and community leaders R.V. and Mamie Wills and Mr. and Mrs. Louis Johnson, owners of Majestic Funeral Home. Veterans of World War II and the Korean War, such as Samuel Pierre Jr. (1929–1952), are buried here as well. (Courtesy of Kenny Kleinpeter.)

Washington Monroe Taylor (born 1870) was pastor of Mount Zion Baptist Church in Baton Rouge as well as several other rural churches around the city. Rev. Gardner C. Taylor stated that his father always believed "there's a better day coming," as he worked for better housing and jobs for all people of Baton Rouge. (Courtesy of Kenny Kleinpeter.)

Epithets are common on mid-20th century tombstones in Sweet Olive, such as, "For me, to live is Christ and to die is gain. Philippians 1, 21" for Rev. Jack Mitchell (1853–1944). The ushers of his church, Shiloh Baptist Church, placed the grave marker in his memory. (Courtesy of Kenny Kleinpeter.)

Other ministers are buried in Sweet Olive Cemetery, including Rev. L.M. Staves (1884–1956), who was a pastor at Green Chapel, according to his simple concrete headstone. The church referred to is possibly Green's Chapel AME Church on North 32nd Street in Baton Rouge. (Courtesy of Kenny Kleinpeter.)

The obelisk in the center is the Sandors family tomb, and behind it is the tomb of Ada Catherine Pollock Blundon (1863–1917). The Sandors obelisk is inscribed, "The Morning Cometh," on one side for John Howard Sandors (1880–1906), and "Safe in Jesus Arms," for eight-month and 14-day-old Francis Sylvester Sandors (1905–1906). Lambs are traditionally used on the tombstones of children. Ada and Frank Blundon were white missionaries from New York who started a school for black children in the late 1880s. Sponsored by the American Baptists, the Live Oak School was located on South Boulevard east of Fannie Street. Blunden's ledger tombstone inscription reads, "This tablet was erected by the colored people of Baton Rouge as a tribute of respect to the twenty nine years of untiring service that she has given to them." Ada Blundon is the only non-African American known to be buried there. Roselawn Monuments restored the Blundon and Sandors memorials, and the Mid City Redevelopment Coalition, Mid-City Cemeteries Coalition, and Roselawn Monuments provided funding. (Courtesy of Kenny Kleinpeter.)

The Sweet Olive Cemetery Association cannot charge enough for burial fees to have funds for repairs. Despite this, some excellent improvements have been made. The portion of America Street that once ran through the cemetery from 22nd Street to Baxter was closed in 1974. Portions of the wall broken by a car accident have been repaired. (Courtesy of Kenny Kleinpeter.)

After years of work for Sweet Olive Cemetery, Fred Cleveland Matthews Jr. died at the age of 95 on October 31, 2001. He and his wife, Vivian Loretta Wills (1910–1989), began the Sweet Olive Cemetery Association in 1975 to preserve and improve the cemetery. They are buried next to his parents. In front of the Matthews tomb are Hatter family graves, which bear the epitaph, "At Rest." (Courtesy of Kenny Kleinpeter.)

W.T. Winfield became president of the Sweet Olive Cemetery after Matthews. He has enlisted cleanup help from the East Baton Rouge Parish Sheriff's Department and the community. This unusual metal covering on a grave was perhaps meant to be covered by some type of tomb. (Courtesy of Kenny Kleinpeter.)

The tombstone in Sweet Olive Cemetery of Dave Terry, born January 30, 1892, and died February 5, 1961, is fashioned by loving hands, not by a professional stone carver. The winged cross symbolizes ascent to Heaven. Folk art is common in cemeteries in the South and Midwest. (Courtesy of Kenny Kleinpeter.)

Throughout Sweet Olive, headstones in the form of an open book are seen, such as the one in the left foreground of this photograph. These symbolize the writing of the deceased's name in the book of life. The three-vault tomb in the background is unusual. (Courtesy of Kenny Kleinpeter.)

Evidence remains that many iron crosses, such as this one, have been lost from Sweet Olive graves. Metal crosses handmade by local blacksmiths were very common in 19th century cemeteries. A number of metal crosses made in the 20th century have been placed in Sweet Olive. (Courtesy of Kenny Kleinpeter.)

The Johnson Family rests in this large, well cared for tomb. Current residents of Baton Rouge have relatives buried in Sweet Olive. Geraldine Brown has a grandmother and a great-grandmother buried there. Edna Jordan Smith, a well-known librarian and genealogist, stated, "my grandmother and her son are here. My great-grandmother, who was a slave, is buried here." Some have grandparents, parents, uncles, and brothers buried in Sweet Olive. (Courtesy of Kenny Kleinpeter.)

Mosaic tile covers the tombstone for an unknown grave. Not until the 1930s did Sweet Olive use vaults, and before that, people were buried in the ground. The cemetery had no regulations about the tombs, so there is much variety. Many are traditional white tombstones, some are covered with tiles, and one from 1965 has tiles decorated with daisies. (Courtesy of Kenny Kleinpeter.)

Five

Magnolia Cemetery

In 1852, the property that was to become the Baton Rouge City Cemetery lay at the outer edges of town. The high, rolling land covered with magnolia and other trees was purchased from John Christian Buhler Jr. for $3,000, and Magnolia Cemetery was established. Although most of the lots were sold to individuals and benevolent societies, one quarter was set aside as a potter's field for the poor and unknown. The 16-acre cemetery was laid out in a rectilinear fashion for lots divided by paths and roads. The original picket fence from 1869 was replaced in installments with an iron fence, which enclosed the cemetery when it was completed in 1909. It was the main burial site for citizens of Baton Rouge, mostly white, but also for some African Americans of prominence. Burials are still allowed for families who own plots.

A few graves from the downtown cemetery were moved to Magnolia Cemetery. Grave markers provide a poignant "who's who" of old Baton Rouge. Some of the heaviest fighting waged during the Civil War Battle of Baton Rouge took place in and near the cemetery. The markers, trees, and picket fence surrounding the cemetery were used as cover by both Confederate and Union troops during the hour-long engagement. Musket and cannon shot caused extensive damage to the site. Eighty-four Confederate and 84 Union troops were killed in the conflict. The next day, after the Confederate troops had withdrawn from the city, local citizens gathered the bodies of the Confederate dead. Although historical records are unclear, local tradition holds that the majority of them were buried in a mass grave within Magnolia Cemetery. Every year, the Foundation for Historical Louisiana's Historic Magnolia Auxiliary Board sponsors a Battle of Baton Rouge Commemorative Ceremony to mark the battle's anniversary. Following the Civil War, due to a poor economy and post-war recovery, and later, as many of the old families moved away, Magnolia Cemetery fell into disrepair. Now listed in the National Register of Historic Places, the cemetery is preserved through the efforts of the Foundation for Historical Louisiana.

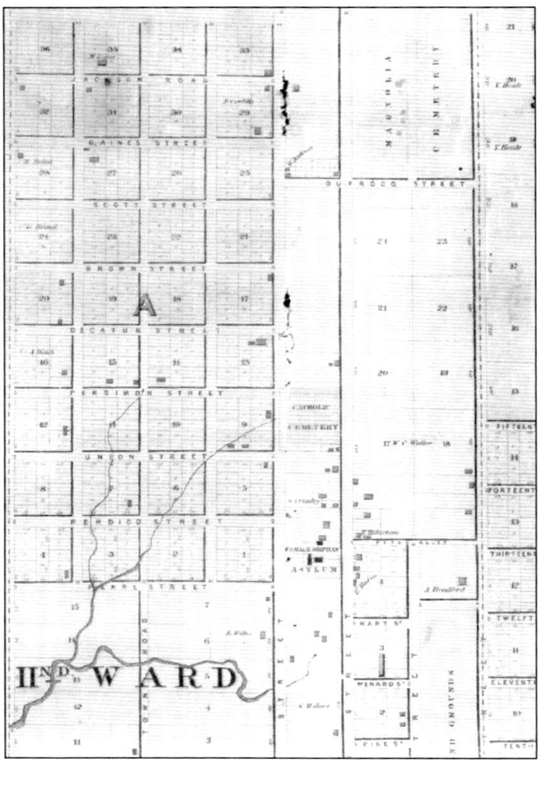

The earliest Magnolia Cemetery entrance sign was replaced in the 1960s. The fence maker misspelled the name as "Magnalia," hence the missing letter in the entrance sign when this photograph was taken. The error has since been corrected. The cast-iron fence encompassing the property was added in 1909. (Courtesy of Martin Gauthier.)

This portion of Michael Gill's 1855 Baton Rouge map shows Magnolia Cemetery in the upper right on Dufrocq Street. One half of the cemetery would become the Baton Rouge National Cemetery after the Civil War. The map also shows the Catholic Cemetery in the center. (Courtesy of the LLMVC, LSU Libraries.)

Nora Dougherty Broussard (1888–1974) and her husband, James Francis (1883–1947), are buried next to her brother Nolan Stewart (1853–1917) and his wife, Lilly McConnell Dougherty (1862–1917). The Doughertys lived in the historic Stewart Dougherty House in downtown Baton Rouge. James Francis Broussard was a well known professor at LSU. (Courtesy of Martin Gauthier.)

Many of Baton Rouge's early citizens, leaders, businessmen, politicians, and families are buried in Magnolia Cemetery. While it was predominately a cemetery for whites, some African Americans are buried there, including Dr. T.A. Walker (1864–1929), Baton Rouge's first African-American physician. His parents were former slaves. (Courtesy of the David King Gleason Collection, LLMVC, LSU Libraries.)

DIED:

At the family residence on the Highland Road, at 11 o'clock a. m. March 5th, 1890,

MRS. E. C. DREHR,

a native of East Feliciana parish, aged 43 years and 3 months.

The friends and relatives of the family are requested to attend the funeral from the family residence to-day (Thursday) at 3 o'clock. The interment will take place at Magnolia Cemetery.

Baton Rouge, La., March 6th, 1890.

Family groupings of graves are common, as with the Swire Family. The earliest of their tombstones seen here is that of Philip Swire (1827–1912) and his wife, Anna Kean Swire (1829–1927). Others in the section are Roger P. Swire and Sadie May Clarke, wife of Stirling B. Swire. Several Woodmen of the World monuments can be seen in the background. (Courtesy of Martin Gauthier.)

Although Mrs. E.C. Drehr (1847–1890) lived closer to the Highland Cemetery, she was buried in Magnolia Cemetery. She was originally from East Feliciana Parish. Although Magnolia did not officially open as the city's cemetery until 1852, it is believed that a private cemetery was operated on the land as early as the 1820s. (Courtesy of the Baton Rouge Funeral Notice Collection, LLMVC, LSU Libraries.)

This is a photograph of Andrew David Lytle's (1834–1917) family plot in Magnolia Cemetery, taken by him. At his death, he would also be buried there. Other family members interred in the plot include his children, Andrew S., William Lundy Lytle (1862–1868), and Howard Lytle (1870–1915), and wife, Mary Ann Lundy Lytle (1836–1898), among others. In 1901, Lytle served as the secretary for the board of directors of the city cemetery. Lytle sadly took the photograph of his son Andrew on his deathbed. Andrew S. Lytle (1857–1859) was born shortly after his parents arrived in Baton Rouge. Of three sons and one daughter, only daughter Ethel (1871–1951) would outlive Lytle. (Courtesy of the Andrew D. Lytle Collection, LLMVC, LSU Libraries.)

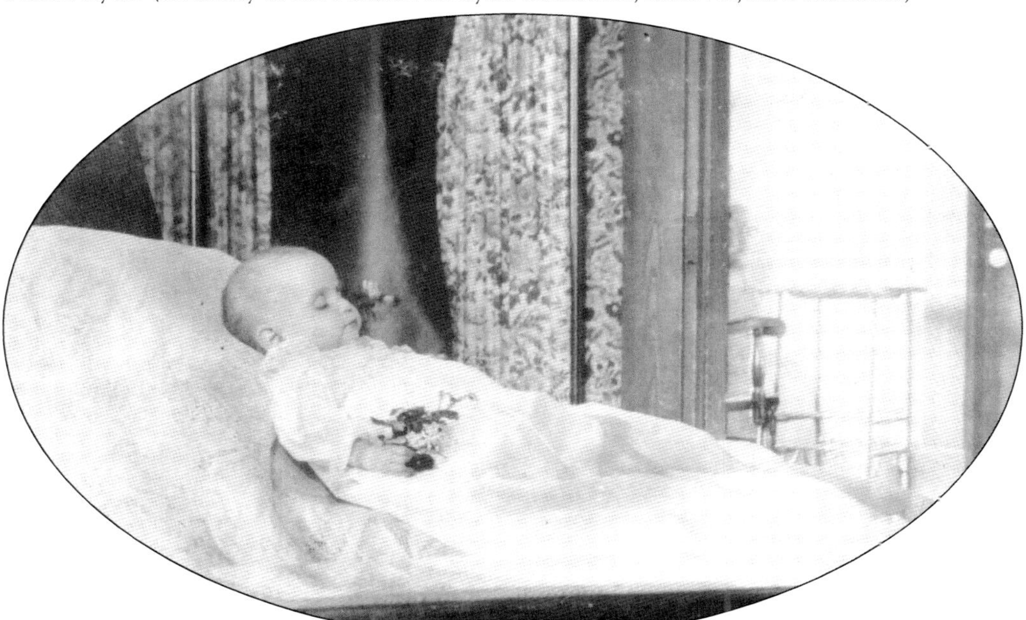

Congressman Thomas Withers Chinn (1791–1852) is buried in Rosedale, Louisiana, but a cenotaph (a monument without a grave beneath) stands for him in Magnolia. Three other congressmen are also buried in Magnolia Cemetery: William Brainerd Spencer (1825–1882); Edward White Robertson (1823–1887), who was also a Confederate veteran; and his son Samuel Matthews Robertson (1852–1911). S.M. Robertson's memorial is a Woodmen of the World roughhewn pillar. (Courtesy of R.C. Albertine.)

The Vince family is watched over by Mother Mary and an angel looking upwards to heaven. Louis Vince's (1837–1934) monument is flanked by the graves of his daughters, Margaret Vince DeJohn (1899–1985), her husband, and Pauline Vince Palazzotto (1902–1975). Louis Vince and his wife, Anna, immigrated to Louisiana from Italy in 1901. (Courtesy of R.C. Albertine.)

In the 1890s and 1900s, horses pulled hearses much like this one, which had two small wheels in the front, two big wheels in the back, and windows on both sides so mourners could see the coffin. They were sometimes called funeral coaches and could be made of elaborately carved wood. (Courtesy of the Foundation for Historical Louisiana.)

Joanna Waddill (1838–1899) is known as the "Florence Nightingale of the Confederacy." She was only 22 when the Civil War began and she volunteered for the Confederate hospital service. She met and married George Waddill while they both tended injured Mississippi soldiers. After the war, the couple moved to George's hometown, Baton Rouge, where they operated drugstores for many years. Both are buried in Magnolia Cemetery. (Courtesy of the Foundation for Historical Louisiana.)

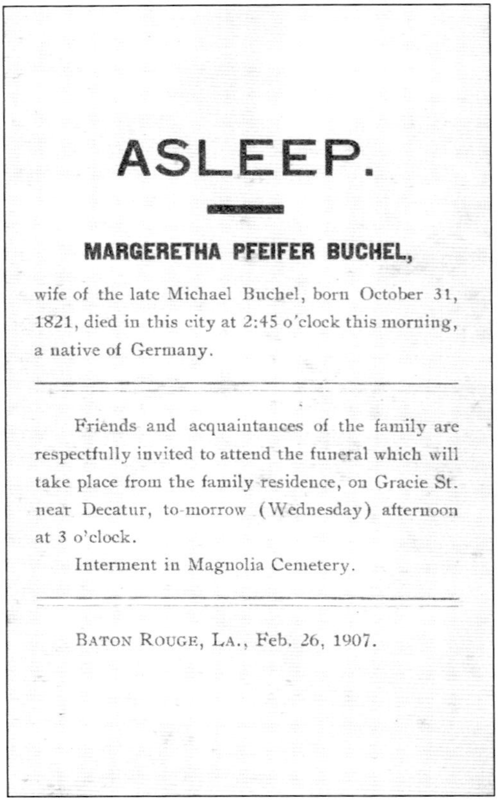

ASLEEP.

MARGERETHA PFEIFER BUCHEL,

wife of the late Michael Buchel, born October 31, 1821, died in this city at 2:45 o'clock this morning, a native of Germany.

Friends and acquaintances of the family are respectfully invited to attend the funeral which will take place from the family residence, on Gracie St. near Decatur, to-morrow (Wednesday) afternoon at 3 o'clock.

Interment in Magnolia Cemetery.

BATON ROUGE, LA., Feb. 26, 1907.

Margeretha Pfeifer Buchel (1821–1907) and her husband, Michael (c. 1814–c. 1868), were immigrants, she from Prussia and he from Baden, Germany. Michael was a butcher, and they had seven children. At the time, announcements of deaths were known as funeral tickets. Many were printed by the local newspaper office and were posted around town the day after a person's death. (Courtesy of the Baton Rouge Funeral Notice Collection, LLMVC, LSU Libraries.)

Dr. Robert Henry Aldrich (born 1867) died November 7, 1906, from a gunshot inflicted by George Kent Favrot (1868–1934). Favrot believed his friend Aldrich had an affair with his wife. Favrot was not convicted of the murder, and in 1921, he was elected to the US House of Representatives. Favrot is buried in Roselawn Memorial Park. (Courtesy of the Ione Burden Family Papers, LLMVC, LSU Libraries.)

Next to the cemetery's fence, which was erected in 1909 and runs along Florida Boulevard, stands a granite obelisk accompanied by a marble angel. Below the monument and lining the expanse of the cemetery on Florida Boulevard is the mass grave of yellow fever victims. The 2008 memorial commemorates the deaths of 114 yellow fever victims who died in 1878. Along the fence on the opposite side was Potter's Field. (Courtesy of Martin Gauthier.)

Sarah Morgan Dawson (1842–1909) is buried in Charleston, South Carolina. Her brothers James and Henry, causalities of the Civil War, are interred in Magnolia. Judge Thomas Gibbs Morgan (1799–1861) and her mother, Sarah Fowler Morgan (died 1871), are also in Magnolia. Sarah is known for the diary she kept during the Civil War destruction of Baton Rouge. Here, Sarah Morgan is portrayed by actress Libby Power. (Courtesy of the Foundation for Historical Louisiana.)

In 2003, the Foundation for Historical Louisiana began "Magnolia's Memories," an outdoor play set in Historic Magnolia Cemetery based on narratives from diaries, military records, logs, history books, and legends. Actors portraying local funeral home operator Charles Ferdinand Rabenhorst and Sarah Morgan as well as photographer Andrew David Lytle are pictured at the Crenshaw Monument. (Courtesy of the Foundation for Historical Louisiana.)

Quiet and stillness are conveyed as moonlight shines upon a cross in Magnolia Cemetery. Modern tombstones, such as this one, are placed side by side with 19th century obelisks, carved angels, urns, and lambs. Burials are still allowed in Magnolia for families that own plots. (Courtesy of the Foundational for Historical Louisiana.)

Funeral laments are played for visitors as well as for the deceased by a bagpiper during the 2003 Magnolia Memories play and tour. Flowers are often carved as adornment on the gravestones in Magnolia Cemetery, as seen here. Laurel leaves represent victory over death. (Courtesy of the Foundation for Historical Louisiana.)

Three children of Methodist minister Rev. William H. Crenshaw and his wife Mary E. Crenshaw died in Baton Rouge's 1858 yellow fever epidemic. Nine-year-old Fanny Bell, seven-year-old Willie Harney, and 18-month-old Mattie Pike are buried in a common grave. The sculpture depicts them. Also in the grave is an infant listed on the tombstone as "The Nameless One," who died in 1855. (Courtesy of the Foundation for Historical Louisiana.)

The Union dead were carried to the other side of what is now Florida Boulevard to land that would be designated the Baton Rouge National Cemetery in 1867. A commemorative ceremony is held every August 5 at Magnolia Cemetery to recall and honor the historic events and to recognize the soldiers lost. Currier and Ives depicted the battle in this 1862 lithograph. (Courtesy of the Library of Congress.)

The Battle of Baton Rouge took place on August 5, 1862. Magnolia Cemetery is the only area of that historic battle that is still intact. In the 1930s, a monument to commemorate the Confederate dead in the battle was erected. Although records are not clear, the Joanna Waddill Chapter of the United Daughters of the Confederacy probably erected it. (Courtesy of the Charles East Papers, LLMVC, LSU Libraries.)

Six

Baton Rouge National Cemetery

Lying in honor are men and women who have fought in America's wars, from the Revolutionary War to the Korean conflict. Listed in the National Register of Historic Places, the Baton Rouge National Cemetery was formally established in 1867, and within two years, 2,925 people had been buried there. Any Union soldier's body located would be buried in the cemetery. At the end of the Civil war, it was reported that the government paid a bonus to anyone who discovered the grave of a Union soldier so that his remains could be reinterred in the national cemetery. It is located one and a quarter miles from the state capitol grounds, adjacent to Magnolia Cemetery on North and Nineteenth Streets. Men from the Civil War Battle of Baton Rouge were the first to be interred.

The brick wall was constructed in 1878 and surfaced with stucco in 1936. The original lodge was located near the main entrance on Nineteenth Street and was replaced in 1931 by a one-story stucco structure. The flagpole is located at the entrance across from the lodge, and a rostrum constructed in the early 1900s is near the center of the cemetery. After the Baton Rouge National Cemetery was dedicated, soldiers from other wars and their families were moved from other cemeteries to it. This cemetery is closed to new interments. However, space may be available in the same gravesite for eligible family members.

Andrew David Lytle photographed the entrance to the Baton Rouge National Cemetery around 1900. Pictured are the original two-story brick lodge and brick wall constructed in 1878. In the background, Magnolia Cemetery can be seen. Before the Civil War, the land on which the cemetery was established was not separate from the city's cemetery, Magnolia. The two were given separate identities in 1867. Both cemeteries have main entrances on North Nineteenth Street. Designed

in an elegant French Second Empire style with a mansard roof, the lodge for the superintendent of the cemetery was similar to those at over 50 other cemeteries. The Baton Rouge lodge was constructed in 1871. The fence was originally wooden, but by 1878 had been improved to brick. (Courtesy of the Andrew D. Lytle Collection, LLMVC, LSU Libraries.)

Lytle stepped closer to the entrance of the Baton Rouge National Cemetery to photograph the original gates, flagpole, gazebo, and gatekeeper's house. Lytle took many photographs of the Union encampments in Baton Rouge during the Civil War occupation. It seems fitting that he also took photographs of the final resting places of many of the soldiers. (Courtesy of the Andrew D. Lytle Collection, LLMVC, LSU Libraries.)

As in Andrew Lytle's life, upright marble headstones mark the graves of the fallen. Only those moved from the downtown military cemetery have flat, ledger-style markers. Inscriptions are limited on the upright markers, but the ledger markers tell more about the individuals buried beneath them. (Courtesy of the Andrew D. Lytle Collection, LLMVC, LSU Libraries.)

Color-lithographed postcards of cemeteries were popular around 1905, when this stylized postcard of the entrance to the Baton Rouge National Cemetery was sold. The lodge shown here would be replaced in 1931 with a one-story stucco structure. (Courtesy of the Leroy Boyd Family Papers, LLMVC, LSU Libraries.)

This is another in the set of 1905 postcards commemorating the Baton Rouge National Cemetery. Cannons as monuments were once prominently displayed in the cemetery. The cannon on the right is near the flat markers of those whose graves where moved from the old fort cemetery downtown. (Courtesy of the Leroy S. Boyd Family Papers, LLMVC, LSU Libraries.)

In memory of Federal Army and Navy soldiers from Massachusetts who lost their lives in the Department of the Gulf during the Civil War, the Massachusetts legislature authorized a monument to be erected in the Baton Rouge National Cemetery in 1909. J.N. White and Sons of Quincy, Massachusetts, constructed it in monumental granite at a cost of $5,000. The 40-foot granite obelisk is probably the most recognized item in the cemetery. Maj. Robert L. Pruyn, who attended the dedication ceremony of the monument, is buried in the Baton Rouge National Cemetery for his service in the Mexican War. He also served in the Confederacy, but that is not noted on his grave. (Courtesy of the Historic American Landscapes Survey.)

The eagle, Massachusetts state seal, and memorial plaque on the monument are made of bronze. The plaque lists the infantry and light battery divisions that participated in the service of the US Army Department of the Gulf. This is the only commemorative monument in the cemetery. (Courtesy of the Historic American Landscapes Survey.)

Union and Confederate veterans came together to honor the men of Massachusetts memorialized by the monument at a dedication ceremony. Pictured from left to right are (front row) Maj. Robert L. Pruyn, veteran of the Mexican War and Confederate Army and mayor of Baton Rouge; and Maj. John McGrath, veteran of the Confederate Army; (second row) St. Clair Favrot, Baton Rouge Confederate veteran; Ebenezer Draper, governor of Massachusetts; and Captain King, superintendent of the cemetery. (Courtesy of the John McGrath Family Papers, LLMVC, LSU Libraries.)

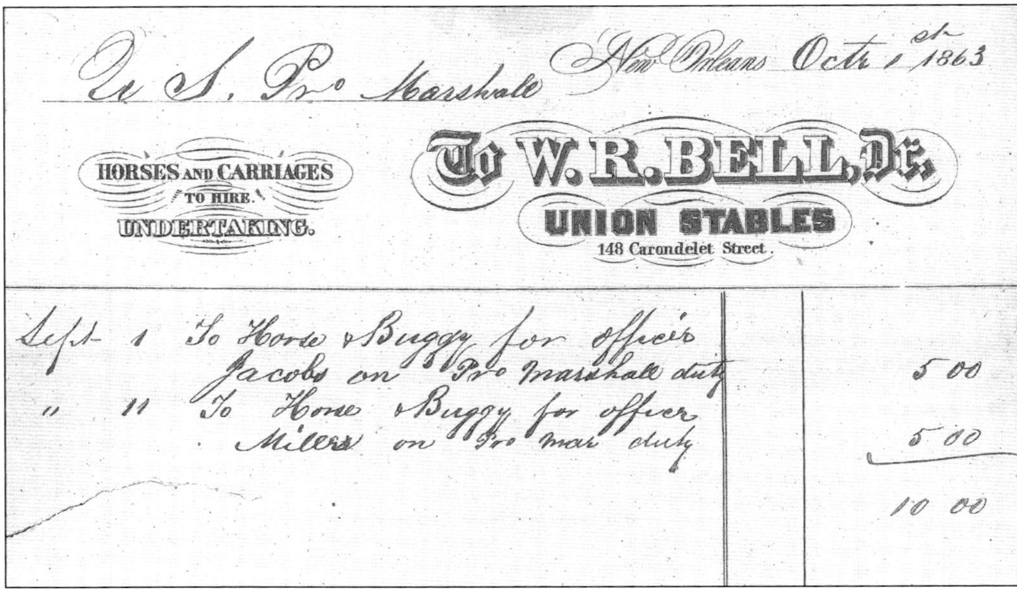

U. S. Pro Marshall — New Orleans Octr 1st 1863

HORSES AND CARRIAGES TO HIRE. UNDERTAKING.

To W. R. BELL, Dr.

UNION STABLES

148 Carondelet Street.

Sept 1	To Horse & Buggy for officer Jacobs on Pro marshall duty		5 00
" 11	To Horse & Buggy for officer Millers on Pro mar duty		5 00
			10 00

Livery stables during the 19th century, such as W.R. Bell of New Orleans, provided horse and carriages for rent for "undertaking," which included transporting the deceased, and if a civilian, the family of the deceased. The US provost marshall was responsible for military interments. (Courtesy of the W.R. Bell Papers, LLMVC, LSU Libraries.)

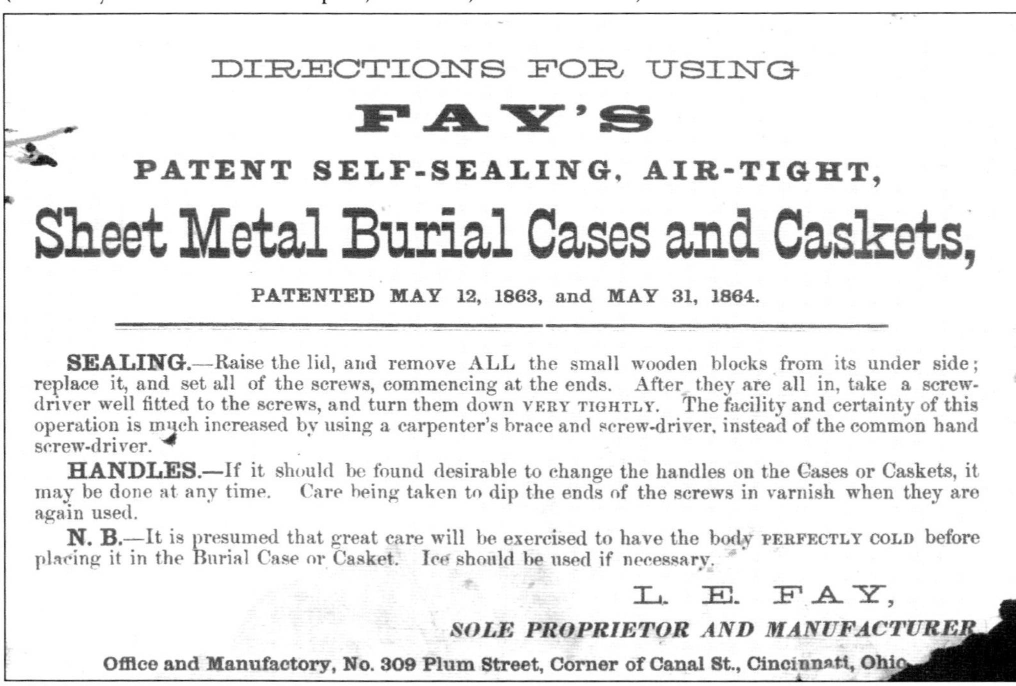

DIRECTIONS FOR USING

FAY'S

PATENT SELF-SEALING, AIR-TIGHT,

Sheet Metal Burial Cases and Caskets,

PATENTED MAY 12, 1863, and MAY 31, 1864.

SEALING.—Raise the lid, and remove ALL the small wooden blocks from its under side; replace it, and set all of the screws, commencing at the ends. After they are all in, take a screw-driver well fitted to the screws, and turn them down VERY TIGHTLY. The facility and certainty of this operation is much increased by using a carpenter's brace and screw-driver, instead of the common hand screw-driver.

HANDLES.—If it should be found desirable to change the handles on the Cases or Caskets, it may be done at any time. Care being taken to dip the ends of the screws in varnish when they are again used.

N. B.—It is presumed that great care will be exercised to have the body PERFECTLY COLD before placing it in the Burial Case or Casket. Ice should be used if necessary.

L. E. FAY,

SOLE PROPRIETOR AND MANUFACTURER.

Office and Manufactory, No. 309 Plum Street, Corner of Canal St., Cincinnati, Ohio.

War led to innovations in munitions, transportation, medicine, and care of the dead. In 1863, manufacturer L.E. Fay of Cincinnati, Ohio, patented a new type of sheet metal casket. The Robert O. Butler family purchased one of the caskets, and these are the directions sent along with it. (Courtesy of the Robert O. Butler Papers, LLMVC, LSU Libraries.)

The federal government purchased seven and a half acres of land for $3,600 in 1867 to serve as the Baton Rouge National Cemetery. It has not been expanded since that time. After the military cemetery was established, remains were brought from the battlefields and military hospitals near Baton Rouge. Remains of Union soldiers from Camden, Arkansas, and Palquemine, Louisiana, were later reinterred in the cemetery. (Courtesy of the Historic American Landscape Survey.)

The octagon-shaped rostrum was completed around 1878. Musicians sometimes performed there and speeches were presented. Few images survive of the cemetery rostrum, or bandstand, in its original construction with a lower section of exposed brick and a galvanized iron roof. The brick was later covered with white stucco, and the iron roof was removed around 1931. (Courtesy of the Andrew D. Lytle Collection, LLMVC, LSU Libraries.)

Andrew David Lytle (1834–1917) is remembered for his many Civil War photographs taken in Baton Rouge. He documented the hardships that the Union and Confederate soldiers encountered. He photographed the Union encampments, their ships, the buildings used as hospitals for the wounded, and the final resting place of those who died. (Courtesy of the Andrew D. Lytle Collection, LLMVC, LSU Libraries.)

After 1932, the rostrum's galvanized roof was removed, but it still invites visitors to linger for awhile. The rostrum, two buildings, the flagpole, and the Massachusetts Monument are the only structures in the cemetery other than the marble markers. Markers are most often adorned with crosses or the federal shield, and the graves face east. (Courtesy of the Historic American Landscapes Survey.)

Thyra Norder and William J. Basler (1873–1938) and other family members often picnicked in the Baton Rouge National Cemetery, which was a popular activity in Baton Rouge in the early 20th century. Mrs. Basler is shown with her niece, Tula Norder, who seems unaware of the camera. (Courtesy of Robert Waltman.)

Rows of evenly placed identical headstones are a testimony of military order extended even to death. A 1987 brochure from the National Cemetery System states its mission: "As a nation, we collectively remember these men and women. Famous or obscure, recruit or five-star general, these veterans gave of themselves to protect the ideals of liberty. They earned the appreciation and respect not only of their friends and families, but of America." (Courtesy of the Historic American Landscapes Survey.)

The poem "Bivouac of the Dead," by Theodore O'Hara, became very popular after the Civil War. Tablets with the poem are found in the oldest cemeteries. At the Baton Rouge National Cemetery, the poem is engraved on a bronze plaque near the rostrum. Seen here in the left of the photograph is the plaque on its concrete base. (Courtesy of the National Historical Landscapes Survey.).

World War I affected many families in Baton Rouge. Alex Hebert, a young solider, was a relative of the Dudley Turnbull Family. The Turnbulls had been free people of color since before the Civil War. The family was Catholic and many of them are buried in St. Joseph's Cemetery. (Courtesy of the Dudley Turnbull Family Papers, LLMVC, LSU Libraries.)

A single central driveway runs the length of the cemetery. Although most headstones are identical, several graves, such as that of World War II Lt. Gen. Troy H. Middleton (1889–1976), who served as president of Louisiana State University from 1951 to 1962, stand out from the rest. (Courtesy of the Historic American Landscapes Survey.)

Alvin Eugene Rabenhorst (1875–1946), a leading Baton Rouge businessman and civic leader, enjoyed photography. He often photographed the Baton Rouge National Cemetery. Andrew Lytle and Rabenhorst both took photographs of the activities they participated in together, such as parades and visits to the cemeteries. (Courtesy of the Alvin E. Rabenhorst Photograph Collection, LLMVC, LSU Libraries.)

Members of the Daughters of the American Revolution often placed memorial flowers on the graves of Revolutionary soldiers buried in the Baton Rouge National Cemetery. They, the Sons of the American Revolution, and the Children of the Revolution chapters also acquired bronze war memorial markers for the graves of those soldiers, such as Philemon Thomas. (Courtesy of the Baton Rouge Daughters of the American Revolution Records, LLMVC, LSU Libraries.)

Early in its history, mounted cannons on each side of the central path marked the entrance to the cemetery. The cannons were subsequently removed. Residents of Baton Rouge enjoyed visiting the cemetery in the 1890s and taking photographs with recently invented Kodak cameras. (Courtesy of the Alvin E. Rabenhorst Photograph Collection, LLMVC, LSU Libraries.)

There were two large gun monuments, such as this one, placed in the central avenue of the Baton Rouge National Cemetery, but they were removed sometime after 1933. A cannonball lies at the base of the monument and another tops it. The plaque at the front of the photograph gives the rules for visiting the cemetery. Visitors were informed that they were not welcome before sunrise or after sunset. If they chose to drive a buggy in the cemetery, "the speed must be confined to a walk." The national cemeteries report of February 1871 stated that three Confederate soldiers were buried in the cemetery. One of those was Robert L. Pruyn. His service in the Mexican War is noted on his tombstone, but his rank as a major in the Confederate Army is not. (Courtesy of the Andrew D. Lytle Collection, LLMVC, LSU Libraries.)

The plaque once affixed to the cannon monument was repositioned onto the new flagpole between 1933 and 1936. The plaque is inscribed, "United States National Military Cemetery Baton Rouge Established 1867 Interments 2936 Known 2442 Unknown 494." The current flagpole is located across the avenue from the lodge and situated on a mound with a six-inch concrete coping in an octagonal shape. (Courtesy of the Historic American Landscapes Survey.)

The main entrance is located on Nineteenth Street at the center of the west side and beginning of the central lane. The entrance is protected by a double iron gate with a pedestrian gate on each side. The historical marker was erected by the city of Baton Rouge. (Courtesy of the Historic American Landscapes Survey.)

Burials of veterans and families in the Baton Rouge National Cemetery have continued since 1868. Permanent plantings, statutes, urns, photographs, or other items are not allowed on the graves. However, seasonal floral arrangements are allowed for 10 days before and after Memorial Day and religious holidays. (Courtesy of R.C. Albertine.)

By 2010, over 5,400 military men, women, and their families were interred within its fence. National cemeteries were established in the United States after the Civil War. Included in the selection criteria for a national cemetery is that the site be of historical interest and convenient to visitors. (Courtesy of the Historic American Landscapes Survey.)

In addition to the front gate, there are two additional gates, one on Convention Street near the utility building and a service gate on the east side along Twenty-Second Street, which was constructed in 1952. Visitors are asked to use the main gate on North Nineteenth Street. (Courtesy of the Historic American Landscapes Survey.)

Seven

Jewish Cemetery and Lutheran Cemetery

The Jewish Cemetery and the Lutheran Cemetery are among the oldest in Baton Rouge. The Jewish Cemetery on North Street dates to 1858. Records in the congregational book of the first Hebrew Congregation of Baton Rouge, Congregation Shaare Chesed (Gates of Loving Kindness), list the first death and burial that year. The 1858 yellow fever epidemic forced the small Jewish community to establish a cemetery association, which acquired land in order to bury the six Jews who had died from the disease. A year later, a small group established a congregation and the Ladies Hebrew Aid Association began to seek a permanent place of worship. By 1885, a building had been purchased for a temple. In August 1886, the name was officially changed to Congregation B'nai Israel (Children of Israel).

The earliest graves in the cemetery known as the Lutheran Cemetery may have been those of slaves from nearby plantations owned by Col. James McCalop and Drs. Henry and Jehu Perkins, known as Richland Plantation. Streets nearby still bear their names. No evidence of a Lutheran Church in the area has yet been found. The name may have been applied to the cemetery because of a benevolent society formed around 1822. In New Orleans, slaves were allowed to buy or be given burial vaults in the Girod Street Cemetery. The slaves formed the Male and Female Lutheran Benevolent Society, and before 1859, the society owned an elaborate society tomb with 70 vaults. The benevolent society tradition could have been brought to Baton Rouge during the decades before the Civil War. Speculation about how the cemetery got its name is easy, but this researcher has not found the facts. The earliest organized church recorded in the area was the Zion Baptist Church, an African-American church, in 1858 or 1859. About three blocks from the Lutheran Cemetery, the McKowen Baptist Church was formed in 1909. Lutheran is located on Eddie Robinson Sr. Drive.

Simon Moyse (1855–1946) and grandson, Hermann Moyse, Jr. (1921–2007) were prominent in Baton Rouge and active members of B'Nai Israel Congregation. Simon was a successful merchant. Hermann would become a banker and veteran of World War II. (Courtesy of the Moyse-Gottlieb-Sommer Family Papers, LLMVC, LSU Libraries.)

Pauline Hirsh, wife of Jacob Kuhn, was born on October 16, 1835, and died on September 23, 1858. Hers was the first recorded death in the organized Jewish community and is the oldest tombstone in the Hebrew cemetery. She and five others died from yellow fever. English, Hebrew, and French inscriptions are found on tombstones in the cemetery. Many times, the word "consort" was used rather than wife. (Courtesy of Martin Gauthier.)

Some of the well-known names in early Baton Rouge retail and banking, such as Tobias, Goudchaux, Gottleib, Rubenstein, and Rosenfield, are found among the tombstones. Former Rabbi Barry Weinstein of B'Nai Israel Congregation said the cemetery was a source of information on Jewish history in Baton Rouge. (Courtesy of Martin Gauthier.)

A postcard of downtown Baton Rouge in 1955 shows some of the store signs of longtime merchants, including Rosenfield's on the left. The buildings date from the late 1880s, but Rosenfield's dates back to 1853. This Rosenfield's store was the first in Louisiana to be completely air-conditioned and have elevators and moving stairs. (Courtesy of the Joseph Simon Family Papers, LLMVC, LSU Libraries.)

The Elgutter family was from Germany and is pictured in 1906 in Baton Rouge. Pictured from left to right are (first row) Ruth Elgutter, an unidentified maid, and Sammy Elgutter; (second row) Adolph, Hilda, and Recha Elgutter. Ruth married into the Rosenbaum Family. (Courtesy of the Max Rosenbaum Family Letters and Photographs, LLMVC, LSU Libraries.)

Grace and Joseph Simon Jr. are pictured around 1920. They were active in the B'nai Israel congregation, encouraging newly arriving Jewish families to join the temple in Baton Rouge. Joseph S. Simon, a watchmaker, and his son Joseph Jr. established a prosperous jewelry store. (Courtesy of the Joseph Simon Family Papers, LLMVC, LSU Libraries.)

Joseph and Rebecca Hahn Gottlieb were philanthropic members of the Baton Rouge community. Their children Lewis Gottlieb and Rosalie Gottlieb Moyse donated their parents' Dreher Avenue home to the United Givers Fund as a headquarters. Lewis served on the 1954 building committee for Temple B'Nai Israel. (Courstey of the Moyse-Gottlieb-Sommer Family Papers, LLMVC, LSU Libraries.)

From their Government Street location, Rabenhorst Funeral Home held services for those of all faiths and at all the historic cemeteries. In business since 1866, they conducted burials in the Jewish Cemetery for the earliest families. They continue to provide services for 21st century Baton Rouge families. (Courtesy of Karen Rabenhorst Kerr.)

Cedar trees in the cemetery have attained dramatic size. These grow well in Louisiana in most types of soil. This photograph also shows examples of double tombs, which are prevalent in the Lutheran Cemetery. The tradition of painting tombs bright colors may have come with slaves from Africa and the Caribbean. (Courtesy of Kenny Kleinpeter.)

In the Lutheran Cemetery, tombs and grave markers are often painted bright colors. Only in recent years were tombs whitewashed. Historically, a lime wash was infused with various colors. In the right foreground is the grave of Bessie K. Ashford, who died on December 21, 1953. Her marker is adorned with the wings of victory. (Courtesy of Kenny Kleinpeter.)

Mary Bell was born in December 1921 and died in November 1966. Her grave is marked with this simple concrete stone in a neglected area of the cemetery. The slope of the ground can be seen in the photograph. The Baton Rouge fault runs west to east from the Mississippi River and is crossed by north to south roads near the cemetery. (Courtesy of Kenny Kleinpeter.)

The topography of this area of Baton Rouge can be seen in the Lutheran Cemetery. Plantations were situated on the natural levees of the Mississippi River, which rose as much as 15 feet above the water line and were a mile or more wide. Land sloped from north to south to the alluvial lowlands. Cemeteries for the plantations were sometimes located on the sloping ground. (Courtesy of Kenny Kleinpeter.)

The marker with the cross in the center of the photograph is for Thompson, but the remaining words are not legible. To the left is the tomb of James Carr, who was born on March 15, 1863, and died May 15, 1953. The marker on his tomb holds the epitaph "Sadly Missed by Wife and Son Oren." (Courtesy of Kenny Kleinpeter.)

These tombs in Lutheran Cemetery are for single burials. When a second person in the family was buried, a separate tomb was added to the top of the old one. Throughout the cemetery, simple, rounded headstones with a cross can be seen. Here also the slope of the ground is clearly seen. (Courtesy of Kenny Kleinpeter.)

The small cross marker is perhaps for the grave of Ross Knot, where his tombstone once stood. It states, "In Memory Our Dear Mother (name unreadable) Ross Knot Sadly Missed by Daughter and Son." Her birth and death dates are unreadable, except for the centuries. She was born in the 19th century and died in the 20th century. (Courtesy of Kenny Kleinpeter.)

Among the old tombs and headstones, the modern granite double tombstone of Corinne Smith stands to the far right. Corinne was born in 1912 and died in 1966. There is no inscription on the left side of the tombstone indicating that it was still vacant when the photograph was taken. (Courtesy of Kenny Kleinpeter.)

Through time and neglect, many headstones in the Lutheran Cemetery are broken and unreadable. Some tombs are sinking down or to one side. Families that once maintained the graves have moved away from Baton Rouge, or no descendants are left. The Lutheran Cemetery still accepts burials, but needs community support for restoration and repair. (Courtesy of Kenny Kleinpeter.)

Graves edge the drive through the cemetery under grand trees, and double tombs appear throughout. On the drive, the whitewashed and painted tombs can be seen. Whether entering or leaving the Lutheran Cemetery, it seems the city is far away, and a visit is worth the time. (Courtesy of Kenny Kleinpeter.)

Eight

Roselawn Memorial Park

Roselawn Memorial Park Cemetery was the first landscaped garden cemetery in Baton Rouge. Roselawn introduced the concept of perpetual care to Baton Rouge in 1921. In the late 1920s, a number of families moved loved ones from St. Joseph's Catholic Cemetery, Magnolia Cemetery, and family cemeteries throughout the parish. When the Roselawn Memorial Park first opened, it was advertised that there would be no need for the individual grave owner to attend to the graves, because Roselawn had a trained staff to take care of all needs relating to the grounds. Magnolia Cemetery was the town's main burial ground in 1921, but Roselawn was to become Baton Rouge's premier cemetery. The American Park Builders, landscape architects of Chicago who also planned the city park, developed the cemetery.

One of the aims of Roselawn was to feature the latest methods of landscape architecture using lawns, hedges, ornamental trees, plants, and winding roadways. The first sales brochure for Roselawn Memorial Park stated that "The morbid features of the old graveyard will not even be a gruesome memory to the visitors to this Modern Park Cemetery, where a tract of land, apart from the outside world, will present to the observer a replica of the most beautiful in Nature." A promotional booklet for Roselawn Memorial Park lists the officers as sales manager H.H. Muma, president A. Grouchy Jr., vice president G.P. McNeel, secretary J.A. DeJong, and treasurer C.M. Downs. In order to encourage members of the parish to move their deceased to Roselawn, the congregation of St. Joseph's Roman Catholic Church printed a number of certificates stating that a member could exchange their lot in St. Joseph's for the same amount of space in "our Roselawn Park Cemetery as per our agreement," on June 23, 1921. The certificates were to the Roselawn Development Association.

Roselawn was built one mile from the 1921 city limits. Fidelity National Bank was named trustee of the cemetery when it opened. It was the first commercial, perpetual care cemetery in Baton Rouge. Families were encouraged to move their deceased loved ones from other cemeteries to the new modern one, and many did. (Courtesy Martin Gauthier.)

The sexton's, or manager's, office was designed by Baton Rouge architect A. Hays Town, who also designed some of the city's most impressive homes. Completed in 1954, its exterior is made of old brick, and its interior is cypress and brick. Town used these features in family homes he designed as well. (Courtesy of Roselawn Memorial Park.)

The third generation of the Rabenhorst family to enter the funeral service business was Alvin Phillips Rabenhorst, shown here with his father, Alvin "Allie" E. Rabenhorst. Allie also began a life insurance company. Alvin Phillips Rabenhorst is buried in Roselawn Memorial Park, as are other members of the Rabenhorst family. (Courtesy of Karen Rabenhorst Kerr.)

A fraction of the purchase price of a plot goes into a fund used to maintain the grounds. The organization responsible for perpetual care, the Roselawn Development Association Perpetual Care Corporation, is separate from the Memorial Park Association. In 1961, Roselawn offered the "pre-need service" to allow families to purchase plots before death. (Courtesy of Martin Gauthier.)

Some of the Sisters of St. Joseph were originally interred in St. Joseph's Cemetery, as were many priests. They were moved to a section in Roselawn Memorial Park devoted exclusively to Catholics. This new memorial to the Sisters in Roselawn has lilies, a symbol for St. Joseph, engraved upon it. Engraved also are the letters "SJ" for Sisters of St. Joseph and the words "Charity and Humility." Two former bishops of the Catholic Diocese of Baton Rouge were moved from Roselawn Memorial Park to the bishops' memorial tomb on the grounds of St. Joseph's Cathedral in 1986. (Courtesy of Martin Gauthier.)

Sabin Gianelloni Sr. (1863–1934) was a successful sugar planter at Longwood Plantation in East Baton Rouge Parish. He emigrated from Corsica to Plaquemine, Louisiana, and in 1892 married Julie Lefebvre (1870–1937) of Baton Rouge. They acquired Longwood Plantation after her father's death. (Courtesy of the Sabin J. Gianelloni, Sr. family papers, LLMVC, LSU Libraries)

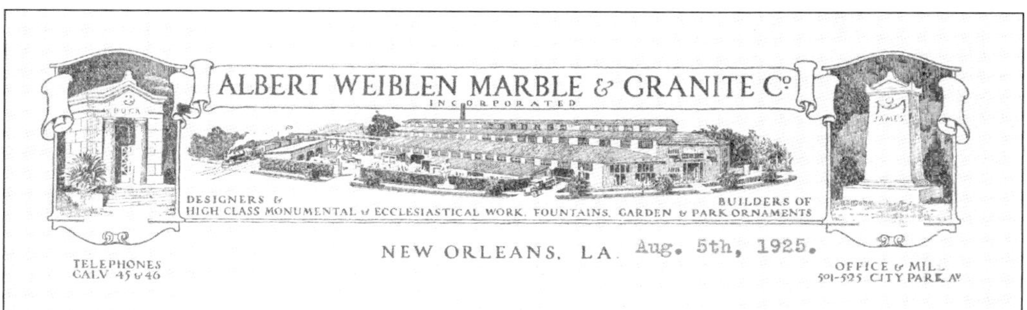

Weiblen Marble and Granite Company of New Orleans drew the plans for the Gianelloni family monument at Roselawn in 1925. They completed the monument after Sabin Gianelloni had approved the plans. The Roselawn Memorial Park Association constructs foundations for monuments such as this. (Courtesy of the Sabin Gianelloni Papers, LLMVC, LSU Libraries.)

Luella M. Fillastre was the first charter member of the Daughters of the American Revolution Baton Rouge Chapter to die. On her grave, the chapter placed the DAR insignia marker, which is in the form of a spinning wheel and distaff. (Courtesy of the Daughters of the American Revolution Baton Rouge Chapter papers, LLMVC, LSU Libraries.)

Officers of the Daughters of the American Revolution Baton Rouge Chapter and the Fillastre family gather to honor Luella Fillastre at Roselawn Memorial Park. The chapter also established a chapter of the Children of the American Revolution in Baton Rouge. (Courtesy of the Daughters of the American Revolution Baton Rouge Chapter papers, LLMVC, LSU Libraries.)

A. Grouchy Jr. was the first president of the Roselawn Memorial Park Association. In 1920, it established offices at 343 Florida Street for pre-opening sales. Officers made clear in their advertisements that religious ceremonies of all faiths were permitted at Roselawn. Grouchy family members are interred at Roselawn. (Courtesy of Martin Gauthier.)

Perpetual care cemeteries, such as Roselawn, provide maintenance of the grounds and provide flowers for purchase by visitors. The first promotional brochure in 1922 stated: "Protective restrictions have been adopted to prevent crowding in order to preserve the symmetry which prevails throughout all Roselawn." In the center of the oak-lined main drive is an evergreen hedge planted and trimmed to form the word "Roselawn." (Courtesy of Roselawn Memorial Park.)

Woodruff's Funeral Home began serving the Baton Rouge community in the 1920s. Their new location in 1943 improved upon the previous one downtown near the railroad tracks. The tasteful sign says simply, "Woodruff's Service." Woodruff's and Rabenhorst Funeral Home were the most well known of the post–World War II Baton Rouge businesses. (Courtesy of the Jasper Ewing Papers, LLMVC, LSU Libraries.)

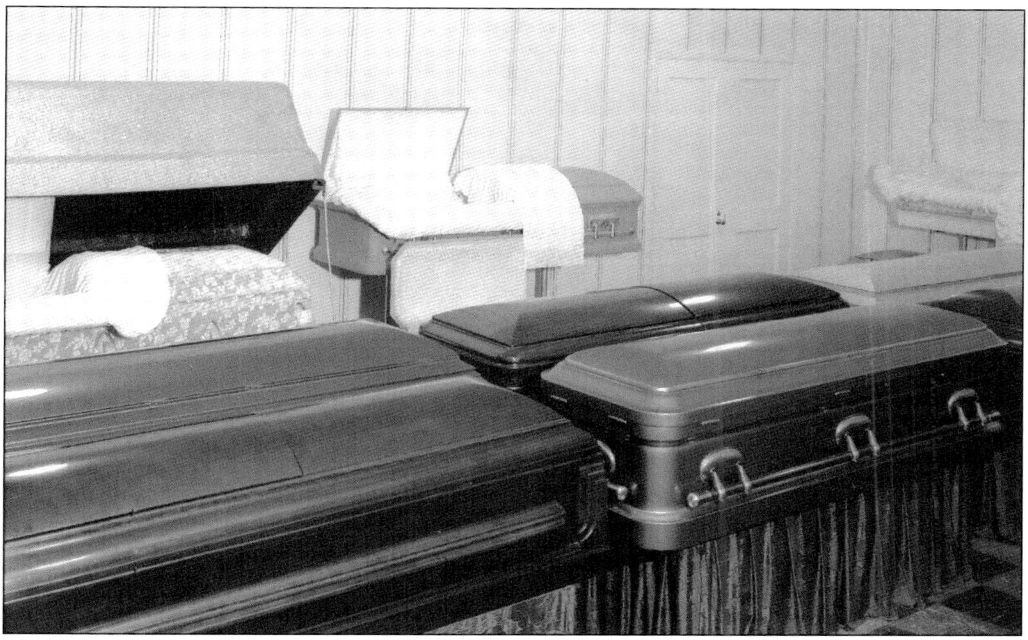

Woodruff's was a full-service funeral home. Displays of new ready-made coffins for families to choose from were considered part of full service. A wide variety of woods and interiors were offered. Custom orders could still be placed if the family desired to do so. (Courtesy of the Jasper Ewing Papers, LLMVC, LSU Libraries.)

The tombstone for Annie Marks (1960–1969) bears her photograph and likeness in the sculpture. Her epitaph states, "Queen of all Angels in Highest Heaven." A gift is placed at her feet. A photograph of an adult woman is also on the tombstone, but she is not identified. These families were Gypsies, and Roselawn Memorial Park has a tradition of Gypsy burials that goes back several generations even though the families are from outside Baton Rouge. Annie's marker stands next to another elaborate tombstone for Miller Marks (1923–1981), who is probably a relative, perhaps her grandfather. (Courtesy of Martin Gauthier.)

Miller Marks's tombstone also has space for his wife, Mary Marks. Even though she had not died when this photograph was taken, her epitaph had already been carved into the stone, "Her life was giving beauty through goodness and love." The epitaph for Miller Marks says, "He was the sunshine in our home." (Courtesy of Martin Gauthier.)

Rabenhorst Funeral Services modernized its fleet of limousines for funeral processions in the 1960s. Funerals to Roselawn Memorial Park often began at Rabenhorst. Roselawn was one mile from the city limits when it opened in 1926, and it was two miles from Rabenhorst Funeral Home on Government Street. (Courtesy of Karen Kerr Rabenhorst.)

Alvin Phillips Rabenhorst Sr. (1916–1977) is buried in Roselawn Memorial Park. He was the grandson of Charles Ferdinand Rabenhorst, who founded Rabenhorst Funeral Home in 1866, and the son of Alvin Eugene Rabenhorst, who started Rabenhorst Life Insurance Company in 1932. All four of his children continued in the family businesses and conducted their father's services at the Government Street location in April 1977. (Courtesy of Karen Kerr Rabenhorst.)

A modern concept for the new building of Welsh Funeral Home around 1960 is shown in this architectural drawing. Welsh Funeral Home would become affiliated with Green Oaks Memorial Park on Florida Boulevard after it opened in 1949. The area was on the edge of town in 1960. (Courtesy of the Jasper Ewing Collection, LLMVC, LSU Libraries.)

A.V. Baskin served as general manager of Roselawn Memorial Park from 1925 until his death in 1958. His nephew James C. Baskin came to work at Roselawn in 1946 as the assistant manager. After his uncle's death, James became the general manager. A.V. Baskin and family are interred at Roselawn. (Courtesy of Martin Gauthier.)

The Saurage family tomb at Roselawn Memorial Park recognizes a prominent business family in Baton Rouge known for their Community Coffee Company. The company is popularly known as CC's. Their industrial operation is at the Port of Baton Rouge west of the Mississippi River in Port Allen. (Courtesy of Martin Gauthier.)

The main shell path into Roselawn Memorial Park winds throughout the cemetery. Roselawn has a mausoleum and columbarium, a vault with niches for urns of cremated ashes. In 2002, the park had 22,000 interred and room to expand for 20,000 more in the 21st century. (Courtesy of Roselawn Memorial Park.)

The Beasley family marker at Roselawn Memorial Park is impressive for its size and rough-hewn granite. To the right is the Stokes family tombstone, and directly behind the older tombstone is that of the Bowman family. To the left are more simple monuments including that of the Jeffreys family. (Courtesy of Martin Gauthier.)

Henry Luse Fuqua (1865–1926) was governor of Louisiana from 1924 to 1926. He was a native of Baton Rouge and operated Fuqua Hardware Company for nearly 40 years. Fuqua served as warden of Louisiana State Penitentiary at Angola from 1916 until he was elected governor in 1926. (Courtesy of the Henry L. Fuqua Papers, LLMVC, LSU Libraries.)

Governor Fuqua died halfway through his term as the 39th governor. He was originally buried in Magnolia Cemetery, but later moved to the newer Roselawn Memorial Park where his grave is marked with this tombstone. He was married to Laura Matta Fuqua (1866–1968), and they had two children, Matta Fuqua and Henry L. Fuqua Jr. (Courtesy of Martin Gauthier.)

The Rabenhorst fleet is shown in front of the state capitol building. These emergency vehicles from Rabenhorst were needed one night in November 1935, when Sen. Huey P. Long was shot in the capitol hallway. Rabenhorst handled the services of the reported assassin Carl Weiss, and Welsh handled Long's services. Weiss was originally buried in Roselawn, but in 1991, his remains were exhumed for investigation and thereafter cremated. (Courtesy of Karen Kerr Rabenhorst.)

Nine

Unique to Baton Rouge

There have been only two state capitol buildings in Baton Rouge, and both are still standing. Each one also has a former governor buried on the grounds. Known as the old state capitol, the 1852 Gothic style castle was abandoned by the Louisiana government in 1862 when Federal forces occupied the city. Union soldiers caused a fire and the building was gutted. It was rebuilt in 1882 for the returning Louisiana government. As a reminder of the Civil War, Gov. Henry Watkins Allen was buried on the grounds in 1885. In 1932, the new state capitol building opened and the old state capitol was once again abandoned. Gov. Huey Long, who built the new capitol, tried to tear down the old castle, but was stopped by a group of determined Baton Rouge women. Unfortunately, the building was neglected for decades until 1991, when a full restoration was begun and the building has been saved, again. After his assassination in November 1935, Governor Long was buried in front of "his" capitol building. His larger-than-life statue looks directly at the capitol. A light shines nightly down from the building onto his statue.

After the Civil War, Gov. Henry Watkins Allen (1820–1866) fled to Mexico in 1865, where he died less than a year later. His body was brought to New Orleans and entombed in Lafayette Cemetery with great ceremony. In 1885, the Louisiana legislature was again under the control of white Democrats, many of whom were Confederate veterans. They paid to bring Allen's remains and his large monument from Lafayette Cemetery to Baton Rouge to be reinterred on the capitol grounds. The monument over his grave was presented to the state by the Allen Monumental Association, which had raised the funds to pay for the monument. (Courtesy of the Andrew D. Lytle Collection, LLMVC, LSU Libraries.)

Lytle photographed Gov. Henry Watkins Allen in his Confederate uniform sometime before the 1862 Battle of Baton Rouge, where Allen was wounded. Lytle also photographed the grave and monument of Governor Allen at the state capitol building in 1885. A statue of Allen is also inside the new state capitol. (Courtesy of the Andrew D. Lytle Collection, LLMVC, LSU Libraries.)

Gov. Huey P. Long (1893–1935), pictured shaking hands with supporters on the capitol steps, was a favorite of Louisiana citizens. Grieving citizens are engraved on the sides of his marble monument, depicting their sorrow at his death. Long was a US senator at the time of his death. (Courtesy of the Huey P. Long Photograph Album, LLMVC, LSU Libraries.)

Huey P. Long served as governor of Louisiana from 1928 until 1932 and as a US senator from 1932–1935. He was assassinated in the capitol building and is buried at the center of the public gardens on the grounds. The marble monument is atop a granite foundation that forms the cap of Huey Long's tomb. A bronze 14-foot statue of Long tops it. The sculptor was Charles Keck (1875–1951), who was known for his monuments of political figures. Long's statue points to a model of the capitol building sculpted into the stone. On the front of the monument is a riderless horse rearing on its hind legs, symbolic of a leader slain in battle. The horse wears a banner that states, "Share the Wealth." This was Long's most recognized social program. A small stone had been placed over the grave before the monument. Now in the Louisiana State Museum, the gravestone is simple granite with the words, "Sleep on Dear Friend and take your rest, they mourn you most who love you best." (Courtesy of the Jasper Ewing Collection, LLMVC, LSU Libraries.)

How to Locate the Cemeteries

1. Begin at the Louisiana State Capitol. View the locations of the military-arsenal cemetery and Our Lady of Sorrows Cemetery.
2. Take State Capitol Drive west to River Road, then go south (turn left) to Government Street, turn east (right) to St. Ferdinand Street, and travel south. St. Ferdinand Street becomes Highland Road. Continue south through the campus of Louisiana State University. Highland Cemetery is 4.8 miles from the state capitol. Turn east (left) off Highland Road on East Parker Boulevard. Turn south (right) on Oxford Avenue, entrance is on Oxford Avenue.
3. Return to Highland and travel north (turn right) to Dalrymple Drive. Go east (right) on Dalrymple Drive to City Park, turn west (left) on East Washington Street, then turn north (right) on Eddie Robinson Sr. Drive. Lutheran Cemetery is on the right at Pear Street, 2.5 miles from Highland Cemetery.
4. Return to Dalrymple Drive and go north (left) until it becomes Park Boulevard. Continue north and cross Government Street where Park Boulevard becomes Nineteenth Street. Continue north on Nineteenth Street. Baton Rouge National Cemetery and Magnolia Cemetery both have entrances on North Nineteenth Street. They are 2.3 miles from Lutheran Cemetery.
5. Return to North Nineteenth Street and go north (right) to North Street, which runs one way west. Turn west (left) on North Street to North Fifteenth Street. The Jewish Cemetery is in the 1400 block of North Street between North Fifteenth Street and North Fourteenth Street, approximately one mile from Magnolia Cemetery.
6. Return to North Street west (right) to North Twelfth Street, turn south (left) to Main Street and turn (left) east (Main Street runs one way east). St. Joseph's Cemetery is at 1500 Main Street less than one mile from the Jewish Cemetery.
7. Return to Main Street and continue east (left) to North 22nd Street, turn south (right). Sweet Olive Cemetery is on South Twenty-Second Street between America Street and Louisiana Avenue. It is 0.8 mile from St. Joseph's.
8. Return to South Twenty-Second Street going north (right) to Florida Street. Follow Florida Street east (right) to Roselawn Avenue (about 1.3 miles). Turn north (left) on Roselawn Avenue, which leads to North Street. Roselawn Memorial Park Cemetery is at 4045 North Street, directly across from Roselawn Avenue and 1.5 miles from Sweet Olive Cemetery.
9. Return to Roselawn Avenue across from the cemetery entrance and go south to Florida Street and turn west (right). Go through downtown Baton Rouge to the Mississippi River Road, turn south (left) on River Road to the Old State Capitol, approximately 3.4 miles from Roselawn. Governor Allen's grave faces the Mississippi River.
10. Return to the River Road, go north (right) to State Capitol Drive approximately 0.7 miles and turn east (right) to the Louisiana State Capitol. Governor Long's statute faces the capitol building.

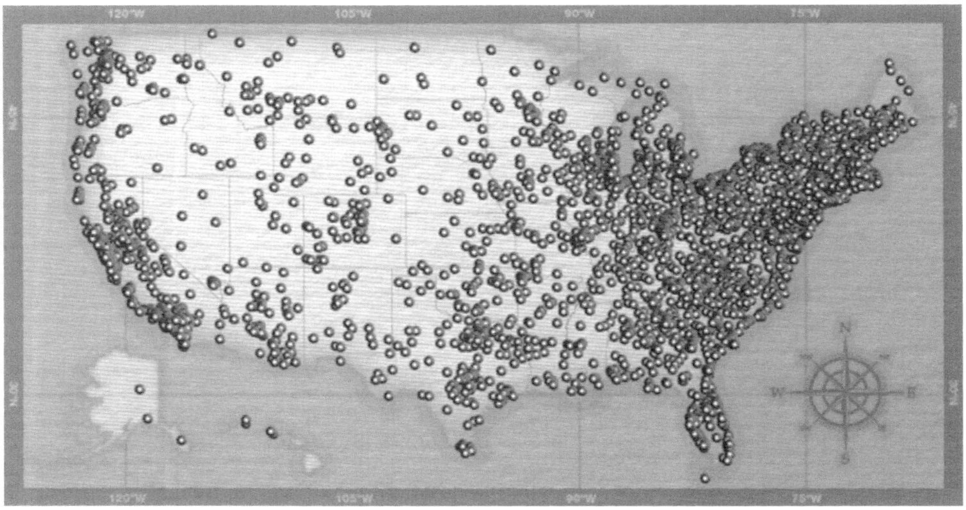

Consistent with our mission to preserve history on a local level, this book was printed in South Carolina on American-made paper and manufactured entirely in the United States. Products carrying the accredited Forest Stewardship Council (FSC) label are printed on 100 percent FSC-certified paper.

MADE IN THE USA